The Civil War is usually regarded as a purely domestic struggle. The essays in *The Union, the Confederacy, and the Atlantic Rim* demonstrate that the conflict was an international event that affected, and was affected by, the policies of many countries.

As fighting between the Union and the Confederacy escalated and both sides sought to engage the sympathies of foreign governments, many countries were forced to grapple with such issues as dependence on Confederate cotton, the nature of de facto independence, new opportunities to expand in Latin America, new techniques of warfare, questions of international law regarding privateers and blockades, and the relations among the European powers themselves.

Continued on back flap

The UNION,
★ ★ ★
the CONFEDERACY,
★ ★ ★
and the ATLANTIC RIM
★ ★ ★

The UNION,
★ ★ ★
the CONFEDERACY,
★ ★ ★
and the ATLANTIC RIM
★ ★ ★

edited by ROBERT E. MAY
★ ★ ★

Purdue University Press
West Lafayette, Indiana

99   98   97   96   95   5   4   3   2   1

The paper used in this book meets the minimum requirements of American
National Standard for Information Sciences—Permanence of Paper for Printed
Library Materials, ANSI Z39.48-1984.

Printed in the United States of America
Design by Cheryl Payne

Library of Congress Cataloging-in-Publication Data
May, Robert E.
        The Union, the Confederacy, and the Atlantic rim / edited by Robert E.
    May
            p.   cm.
        Includes bibliographical references (p.   ) and index.
        ISBN 1-55753-060-2 (cloth : alk. paper) — ISBN 1-55753-061-0
    (paper : alk. paper)
            1. United States—Foreign relations—1861–1865. I. Title.
    E469.M38 1995
    327.73—dc20   94-32424
                                                                              CIP

To Jill

★   ★   ★

CONTENTS

★   ★   ★

PREFACE

★ ★ ★

The ghost of a distinguished historian haunts this collection of lectures about the diplomacy of the American Civil War. Certainly Louis Martin Sears (1885–1960), whose bequest to Purdue University provided for a lecture series and visiting professorships in U.S. diplomatic history, would have appreciated the 1994 lecture series theme, "The Union, the Confederacy, and the Atlantic Rim."

Sears, a professor at Purdue from 1920 to 1956, had amazingly eclectic research interests. Modern scholars tend to be products, and perhaps victims, of academia's inclinations toward specialization. But Sears, a diplomatic historian, displayed an inspirational catholicity in his research tastes. His textbook (*A History of American Foreign Relations,* 1927), several monographs, and more than thirty scholarly articles, book chapters, and other publications ranged widely through the U.S. diplomatic experience from the early republic through the world wars.

Still, Sears, especially during his early professional career, could not resist the spell that the Civil War has cast on this country's historians.

James M. McPherson, noting the more than fifty thousand titles about that conflict, has observed that the Civil War is the "most written-about event in American history." Sears contributed to this national obsession.

Sears wrote two articles that treated French responses to the Civil War. He authored a spirited piece about August Belmont, the banker and former U.S. diplomat who undertook an unofficial overseas mission for the Union. Sears's biography and articles about John Slidell related that Louisiana politico's mission as Confederate commissioner at the court of French emperor Napoleon III. He edited letters penned and received by the London *Times'* special American correspondent, William H. Russell, during the formative stages of the Confederacy and the war's first year. And his textbook devoted an entire chapter to Civil War diplomacy. There, Sears gave vent to what today would be dismissed as a pro-Union bias. He used words like "we" and "our" to describe Union diplomacy, and exulted over Union secretary of state William H. Seward's exemplary management of foreign relations. Sears expressed gratitude that the Union's "happy" selection of diplomats counterbalanced its sorry reliance on bungling military commanders.

So we can safely assume that Sears, were he still alive, would be pleased that the lectures offered in his name have, for the first time, treated the Civil War. Hopefully, too, he would be inspired, as I have been, by the fresh perspectives that Howard Jones, R. J. M. Blackett, Thomas Schoonover, and James M. McPherson, the 1994 Sears lecturers, have brought to the engrossing story of that conflict's diplomacy.

This volume not only reproduces these lectures with their accompanying documentation but also includes transcripts of the question-and-answer sessions that immediately followed each lecture. During these sessions, the speakers amplified upon some of their comments and addressed matters of Civil War diplomacy not covered in their formal remarks.

Thanks are due to my department head, John J. Contreni, and my colleagues on the Purdue University Department of History's Sears Lectures Committee for endorsing the Civil War theme and for encouraging publication of these lectures. I am especially indebted to Purdue professors Vernon Williams and Patrick Hearden for their assistance in selecting the 1994 Sears lecturers, and to the Department of History's secretarial and clerical staff for help in preparing this manuscript for publication.

INTRODUCTION

★ ★ ★

ROBERT E. MAY

The Civil War is usually remembered as a purely domestic struggle. Americans fought their fellow countrymen, or, as Confederates believed, their former fellow countrymen, at sites on U.S. soil such as Shiloh, Antietam, and Gettysburg or on waters just offshore such as Hampton Roads and Mobile Bay. Yanks battled Rebs. Foreign nations, except for the thousands of immigrants that they supplied to Union and Confederate ranks, had no role in *our* Civil War.

Unfortunately, such impressions play havoc with history, for the conflict, from its very inception, was an international event. It most affected European and Latin nations and dependencies on the Atlantic rim but also had repercussions in lands as far away as British India and Tsar Alexander II's Russia. Decisions by foreign governments, in turn, influenced the course of the Civil War.

Foreign peoples closely followed the outbreak of war in North America in the spring of 1861. For one thing, to some opportunistic foreign leaders, the Civil War represented a unique opportunity to increase the territory and influence of their own countries. In the 1850s, the United States had been an aggressively expansionist nation, not only securing the Gadsden Purchase from Mexico and making attempts to acquire the Spanish colony of Cuba but also demonstrating more determination than in the past to champion the Monroe Doctrine's proscription against new European colonies in the Western Hemisphere. In response to pressure from the United States, Great Britain agreed to withdraw from several of her Central American holdings in the 1850s. However, the division of the Union and the creation of the Confederacy in the winter of 1860–61, and the subsequent outbreak of war, promised to absorb American energies so completely that the United States would be unable to commit the naval and other resources necessary to forestall European initiatives in Latin America.

In early 1861, as Abraham Lincoln wrestled with the status of Fort Sumter and other policy decisions relating to the secession crisis, Spain reannexed a former New World possession—the Dominican Republic (also known as Santo Domingo). Later, while the Civil War was raging, French troops captured Mexico City, gained control over roughly half of Mexico, and imposed a puppet government headed by Austrian Archduke Ferdinand Maximilian upon those areas of Mexico under French control. While both these initiatives were in the works well before the Civil War erupted, it is possible that neither of them would have been carried through had there not been a Civil War to distract the United States. In answer to British cautions that the United States might resist the Spanish intervention in Santo Domingo, one Spanish official answered, "The United States of today are very different from that they were a year ago; they have differences of their own to settle." The assessment was accurate. Although the Lincoln administration expressed dissatisfaction with these European initiatives, it was hardly in a position to do anything substantive to reverse them, even in alliance with other countries. When, in 1862, Peru and several other Latin states approached the administration with proposals for resistance against the French intervention in Mexico, Union secretary of state William H. Seward declined cooperating with the movement. Nor was resistance forthcoming from a Confederate government anxious to curry favor with European countries.[1]

Europeans, moreover, felt compelled to ponder the military meaning of the Civil War. They had not witnessed fighting on such a grand scale since the Napoleonic Wars. European policymakers wondered how the transportation of troops by railroad, which occurred in warfare for the first time during the Civil War, would affect their own future military operations. How would field telegraphs, observation balloons, ironclad warships, breech-loading rifles, hand grenades, rifled artillery, and land mines—all initiated or widely used for the first time in the Civil War— change the way their generals would plan and execute future campaigns? Did Civil War changes in cavalry tactics and the tendency of Union and Confederate soldiers to dig battlefield entrenchments indicate new norms in warfare? Great Britain, France, and Prussia, Europe's leading industrial and military powers, sent official observers to witness the war. So did Switzerland. Other Europeans crossed the Atlantic as unofficial observers or as newspaper or journal correspondents. Many penned extensive accounts of their impressions. Lieutenant James Arthur Fremantle, on leave from Britain's Coldstream Guards, for example, passed three months in the Confederacy in 1863 before entering Union lines. He witnessed both the battle of Gettysburg and the New York City draft riots, then returned to Britain and published an account of his experiences later that year.[2]

Most importantly, foreign governments had to make policy decisions regarding the Civil War that not only affected their own nations' welfare but also had the potential to affect the war's ultimate outcome. No sooner had the Confederate States of America been organized in February 1861 than foreign leaders had to weigh the implications of granting Jefferson Davis's government official recognition. According to international law, governments merit recognition when they establish their *de facto* independence. But what constituted *de facto* independence for the Confederacy? Did Southern military victories, such as in the first battle of Bull Run (21 July 1861), indicate that Confederate nationhood had been achieved? Perhaps. But Lincoln's Union government denounced the Confederacy as the result of rebellion, and invariably resumed its military pressure on the southern armies following Union defeats on the battlefield. Furthermore, Union officials, most especially Seward and Union minister to Great

Britain Charles Francis Adams, warned foreign governments that recognition of the Confederacy invited war with the Union. The recognition question, therefore, was fraught with complications.

Not only did foreign leaders have to respond to Confederate claims to diplomatic recognition, which were pressed by Confederate diplomats in London, Paris, Madrid and Brussels,[3] but they also were compelled to develop policies as the Civil War at sea unfolded. How should they respond to Davis's 17 April 1861 proclamation and a subsequent act by the Confederate Congress authorizing privateers to prey on Union merchant and government vessels? The Confederate decision to authorize privateers was a natural one, given the Union's control of almost all of the prewar United States Navy. But the Confederate policy raised difficult problems for foreign governments. Should ships operating under Confederate "commissions of marque and reprisal" be allowed to bring their prizes into European harbors for adjudication before prize courts? Or should foreign countries treat the officers and crews of Confederate privateers as pirates, as the Lincoln administration wished? According to international law, privateers were considered auxiliaries of governments at war and entitled to profits from cargoes they captured. Piracy, on the other hand, was punishable by death. More than forty nations, including Britain, France, Austria, and Prussia, had signed the Declaration of Paris (1856), outlawing privateering, but since the United States had never initialed the pact, the Confederacy seemed unfettered by its provisions.[4]

Likewise, foreign leaders had to react to the Lincoln administration's announcements in April 1861 that it intended to impose blockades upon Confederate ports. Should foreign governments respect a Union blockade of the Confederacy, even though the North for some time lacked anything approaching the number of vessels required to consistently prevent access to Confederate ports? According to international law, countries were not required to recognize ineffective, or "paper," blockades. But failure to accede to the blockade risked war with the Union.

Foreign governments, therefore, could not avoid becoming a part of the Civil War story. In fact, one can even make the case that there might never have been a Civil War had not many southerners calculated on playing a "foreign card" if northerners militarily contested their states' decisions to leave the Union and form the Confederacy.

Southerners believed that the economies of Great Britain and France depended upon shipments of their cotton. Since 1796, when southern cotton upstaged Indian varieties in European markets (it was cheaper and superior in quality), Europeans had come to rely upon shipments from the slave states. Prior to the Civil War, the South had provided more than three fourths of Britain's cotton imports. In 1858 American cotton amounted to 732,403,840 of the 931,847,056 pounds of the raw fiber brought into Great Britain. Furthermore, textiles had become Britain's most important industry, with cotton goods providing from two fifths to five ninths of her exports. Her textile mills and related industries and trades employed massive numbers of workers, including people such as the stevedores and warehousemen who handled cotton when it arrived at British docks. According to one contemporary estimate, four million of the twenty-one million people living in England, Ireland, Scotland, and Wales in one way or another depended upon cotton production.[5]

What would happen if war interrupted the flow of Dixie's cotton to European nations? Many southerners wrongly, but not irrationally, anticipated this scenario: European mills would shut down, throwing massive numbers of desperate people onto the streets; social and political unrest would be the inevitable result; and to preempt revolution at home, European governments would have to rescue the Confederacy so that the cotton trade might resume. In 1858, James Hammond, U.S. senator from South Carolina, proclaimed to his northern colleagues that they would never dare wage war on the South because cotton was "King." Hammond predicted that if the cotton flow were severed for a mere three years, "England would topple headlong and carry the whole civilized world with her." Such assumptions persisted into the early Confederacy, as English correspondent William H. Russell discovered when he showed up in Charleston, South Carolina, days after the surrender of Fort Sumter. "The doctrine of 'cotton is king,'" he observed, "to them is a lively all powerful faith. . . . Here were these Southern gentlemen exulting in their power to control the policy of Great Britain."[6]

Southerners first experienced disappointment regarding their diplomatic expectations in the late spring of 1861, when major European powers, instead of granting immediate recognition of the Confederacy, announced their intention to avoid involvement in the Civil War. Queen Victoria proclaimed Britain's neutrality on 13 May. Emperor Napoleon III's France followed suit on 10 June. Spain did so a week later. Furthermore, European governments defined their neutral obligations in ways that worked to the Confederacy's disadvantage. For instance, France's proclamation of neutrality put a limit of twenty-four hours on the time that Union or Confederate privateers with captured prizes could spend in French ports, and did not allow such privateers to sell their prizes while in France. Since the Union did not need privateers to wage naval war on the South, while the South was dependent on such vessels to wage war at sea against the North, such limitations clearly worked to the Union's benefit.

Foreign leaders and diplomats occasionally held informal meetings with Confederate officials and diplomatic representatives, especially during the early stages of the war. Confederate diplomats managed to secure two unofficial audiences in early May 1861 with Lord John Russell, foreign secretary in the British Cabinet headed by Prime Minister Lord Palmerston. By mid-July 1861, they had also arranged meetings with French foreign minister Edouard Thouvenel and Charles Louis Joseph Morny, the illegitimate half-brother of Emperor Napoleon. But little of a tangible nature resulted from these meetings, and some southerners already wondered whether their hopes of European aid had been a delusion. "Oh if England & France are against us! My breath is stopped," Mary Chesnut despaired in her diary.[7]

Lincoln's administration was by no means itself pleased with the initial European position on the war. By proclaiming neutrality, European nations recognized the Confederacy's belligerent status, which meant that the Confederacy had the right to arrange loans and buy arms abroad. Still, the danger of direct European involvement in the conflict, and the boost to Confederate morale that would have resulted from formal recognition by foreign nations, had been averted, at least for the time being.

Confederate hopes for foreign recognition and aid, however, survived these initial setbacks. For one thing, the Union Congress passed a series of wartime hikes in the United States tariffs on imports, alienating various interests in Britain with rates that by the war's end were more than twice as high as they had been in 1857. More importantly, it took time for "king cotton" to truly come into play, partly because the Confederate government never enacted an absolute prohibition of cotton shipments abroad, partly because of holes in the Union blockade, and partly because large amounts of cotton had been stockpiled in Europe prior to the announcement of the Union blockade. When, by the fall of 1862, a "cotton famine" seemed to sweep over Britain's textile districts, Confederate diplomatic prospects brightened. That autumn, almost 75 percent of Britain's mill laborers found themselves either unemployed or reduced to light schedules. French and Belgian textile production also declined, throwing laborers out of work or on short time. Furthermore, other sectors of European economies were also hurting because of the Civil War's disruption of normal trade: French exports of porcelain, silk, gloves, and many other products fell off sharply during the Civil War.[8]

Incidents at sea, especially the "*Trent* Affair," also held the potential to cause European involvement in the war. This incident began on 8 November 1861, a little more than a half year after the fighting started, when Union captain Charles Wilkes, commanding the sloop *San Jacinto*, stopped the British mail-packet *Trent* on its way from Cuba to St. Thomas in the Danish West Indies (today the Virgin Islands). Wilkes intercepted the *Trent* because its passengers included James M. Mason and John Slidell—recent appointees as Confederate commissioners to Great Britain and France, respectively. He fired two shots across the *Trent*'s bow, forcing the vessel to heave to, had a lieutenant and some marines remove Mason, Slidell, and their secretaries, and took the captured diplomats to Boston, where they were imprisoned at Fort Warren. Wilkes justified the seizure by the logic that nations at war, according to international law, could seize contraband (that is, goods considered useful to an enemy's war effort) being carried by neutral ships. In this instance, he contended, Mason and Slidell constituted contraband of war because they embodied Confederate dispatches.[9]

Wilkes believed that he had struck a great blow for the Union cause, and at a time when Union land forces had yet to win a significant battle. Instead, he brought his country to the brink of war with Great Britain. British leaders and much of British public opinion interpreted Wilkes's seizure of Mason and Slidell as a hostile act and a violation of international law. Persons had not previously been recognized as contraband under international law. Furthermore, Wilkes had not adhered to established procedures in disposing of contraband according to international law, even if Mason and Slidell did qualify. Wilkes should have confiscated the *Trent* and its entire cargo and taken it to port for adjudication in a prize court. International law acknowledged prize courts as the appropriate forum for determining whether given cargoes were indeed contraband and liable for seizure. Instead, he had allowed the *Trent* to proceed on its way.

After learning of Wilkes's act and arranging a united response with French leaders, the British government presented the Lincoln administration with demands that the United States apologize for Wilkes's act, provide reparations for the deed, and release Mason and Slidell. Foreign Secretary Russell instructed Lord Richard Lyons, British minister to Washington, to return to London if the Union government did not agree to British demands within a week—indicating that Palmerston's government was prepared to sever diplomatic relations with the United States over the incident.

With war talk in the air on both sides of the Atlantic, British leaders undertook preparatory military steps. Since Britain's North American Provinces, today's Canada, offered a likely target for Union attacks should war occur (invasions had occurred in both the American Revolution and the War of 1812), British leaders sent 11,175 soldiers on eighteen transports to reinforce the Provinces. The *Toronto Leader,* the most outspokenly pro-Confederate organ north of the border, called for the mustering of militia and warned that the Provinces would crush the North.

Fortunately for the Union cause, Lincoln and Seward, after some bluster and indecision, had the sense to release Mason and Slidell, concede that Wilkes had erred by not taking the *Trent* before a prize court, and agree to reparations. These concessions proved sufficient to defuse the crisis, even though the Lincoln administration denied Britain a formal apology for the affair and Seward sustained Wilkes's contention that persons could constitute contraband.[10]

Not only did incidents at sea threaten European intervention in the Civil War, but so did occurrences on land. Certainly the "St. Albans Raid" of 19 October 1864 had this potential. In this raid, a force of between twenty and twenty-two men serving under Confederate lieutenant Bennett H. Young, in a plot hatched by Confederate agents operating in British North America, used the province of Canada East as a base to attack St. Albans, Vermont, just across the border. The small band robbed banks, killed a town resident and wounded another, and unsuccessfully tried to set St. Albans on fire before fleeing northward and recrossing the border.

The incident took a dangerous turn for Anglo-Union relations because of Union violations, and anticipated violations, of British neutrality following the raid. Not only did a posse of Vermonters commanded by a captain on leave from the Union army cross the border into Canada East in pursuit of the raiders, but Union general John A. Dix, commander of the Military District of the East, issued two orders calling on federal troops to cross the border. The second of these orders, issued after some of the raiders had been captured by the posse, handed over to Canadian authorities, and then released on technicalities by a police magistrate in Montreal, called on Union troops to bring the perpetrators back to the United States for military trial and specified that they should not be surrendered to Provincial authorities. Over in England, Lord Russell, appalled by Dix's blatant disregard for British sovereignty and neutrality, warned Adams that Dix's order played into Confederate hands. On 17 December 1864, Lincoln revoked Dix's most recent order, lessening the tension. However, Robin Winks, in a thorough study of U.S.-Provincial relations during the Civil War, suggests that had this same incident occurred in 1861, when the Confederate cause seemed promising, rather than in 1864, when Union victory appeared imminent, it probably would have triggered British intervention in the Civil War. Enough fear of Union invasion persisted afterwards in British North America that the Canadian Parliament, in early 1865, gave added attention to a project already in the works to unite the several provinces in a Confederation of Canada. The fusion in 1867 of four of the provinces in a Dominion of Canada, under the British North America Act, constituted a vital step toward complete Canadian independence (which occurred in 1931) and may have been the most tangible international repercussion of the American Civil War.[11]

While awaiting a breakthrough on the diplomatic front, in April 1861, the Davis administration assigned army captain Caleb Huse to "special service" abroad as a Confederate procurement agent. Despite a number of obstacles—such as a proclamation by Queen Victoria in December 1861 against the export from Britain of arms and ammunition and a sharp plunge in the value of Confederate credit after news arrived in Europe of the Federal capture of Vicksburg on 4 July 1863—Huse and other Confederate agents succeeded in purchasing considerable quantities of munitions for the Confederacy. Initially using the small amount of gold and silver coin (specie) that was available in the Confederacy and put at their disposal, and later relying heavily on borrowing expedients (such as the sale of certificates that entitled bearers to run the Union blockade and collect a stipulated amount of cotton at specified Confederate ports), Huse and company acquired artillery, small arms, gunpowder, shovels, axes, and countless other items—even the paper for maps and Confederate treasury notes. Some of these supplies entered Confederate ports on British-built and manned blockade-runners, which led to further Anglo-Union tension in instances when Union blockading vessels seized privateers and Union authorities then imprisoned the crews.[12] Other supplies entered the Confederacy through Mexico. Since the Union navy could not blockade the coast of a friendly power without committing an act of war, goods made their way to the Confederacy via river traffic from the Gulf of Mexico to Matamoros, Mexico, and then by transit across the Rio Grande to Brownsville, Texas. When Union army forces occupied Brownsville from November 1863 to July 1864, the trade shifted west to Laredo and Eagle Pass.[13]

Far more consequential than munitions purchased abroad, however, was the Confederacy's ability to buy English-built cruisers and blockade-runners despite British restrictions against such sales. Using all sorts of subterfuges, Georgian James D. Bulloch—a former U.S. naval officer and merchant marine captain—and other Confederate agents were able to acquire such vessels, sneak them out of Britain, and put them in the service of the Confederacy. The cruiser *Florida* captured or sank thirty-six Union ships between August 1862 and October 1864. The *Alabama's* totals were sixty-six ships taken as prizes or sunk. The *Shenandoah* captured more than forty ships—some of them whaling ships taken in the Bering Straits in the summer of 1865, after the Civil War had ended. The *Tallahassee,* a sometime blockade-runner turned cruiser that adopted a succession of names during her Civil War career, took twenty-nine Union vessels. Additionally, in the early summer of 1862, Bulloch contracted with William Laird and Sons Company of Birkenhead, the same builders who constructed the *Alabama,* for two ironclad rams. Loaded with technological innovations, these vessels were specially designed to destroy Northern monitors and break up the Union blockade. In addition, by mid-July 1863, Bulloch had signed contracts with Lucien Arman, France's largest shipbuilder, for the construction of six warships for the Confederacy.[14]

In the end, of course, Confederate leaders came up far short of their foreign-policy goals, though they kept trying new initiatives throughout the war, including the sending of a chaplain in the Confederate army, John Bannon, to deal with the pope. Confederate agent José Augustín Quintero, a bilingual Cuban, managed to extract the offer of an alliance from Santiago Vidaurri, governor and caudillo of the northern Mexican states of Nuevo León and Coahuila. But no major foreign power ever granted the Confederacy diplomatic recognition.[15]

As early as August 1863, only a little more than halfway through the Civil War, a highly frustrated Judah P. Benjamin (Confederate secretary of state from March 1862 until the end of the war), despairing of the Confederacy's ever achieving British recognition, ordered Mason and his secretary to leave London and "consider your mission at an end." Two months later, British customs officers seized the "Laird rams." Thereafter, British policy regarding what Lord Russell termed the "so-called Confederate Government" became ever more unfriendly.

Confederate hopes for a breakthrough with Napoleon III, who, as Benjamin put it, "professed an earnest sympathy" for Dixie's cause throughout the war, persisted longer. As late as November 1864, Slidell hoped that French anger over the Union navy's infringement of Brazilian neutrality when it captured the Confederate cruiser *Florida* in Brazilian waters might "bring about our recognition, and perhaps to substantial intervention in our behalf."[16] But Slidell was engaging in wishful thinking. The French government even clamped down on shipbuilding for the Confederacy. The only French-built warship that made it into Confederate hands was the ironclad *Stonewall,* and it did not arrive at the southern coast until a month after Lee's surrender.

As for Confederate diplomacy with Russia, it never got off the ground. The Davis administration had to recall its appointee as commissioner to Russia even before he reached St. Petersburg because the Confederate Senate had so little faith that the mission could accomplish anything that it never confirmed the appointment.[17]

Nothing better exposed the ultimate bankruptcy of Confederate diplomacy more clearly than the "Kenner mission"—the Confederacy's desperate attempt to wring last-minute recognition and intervention out of the European powers. In January 1864, Confederate general and Irish native Patrick Cleburne, in a letter to General Joseph Johnston, commander of the Army of Tennessee, noted England's hostility to slavery and proposed that the Confederacy arm blacks and relinquish slavery in order to secure independence. In one of the most bizarre twists in American history, the Confederate government—a government formed primarily for the purpose of defending slavery against perceived threats from Lincoln and other antislavery northerners—over the course of the next year moved slowly toward embracing this very expedient. And while this process was unfolding, Davis, in December 1864, decided to send Louisiana sugar planter and slaveowner Duncan F. Kenner, a representative in the Confederate Congress, to Europe to offer a trade of emancipation for recognition or intervention.

Slidell presented Kenner's proposal to Napoleon III, but the emperor evaded a response by indicating that he would not act without prior agreement on a joint recognition policy from Britain. On 14 March, Mason, who had joined Slidell in Paris after the termination of his mission but traveled back to London to conduct emancipation diplomacy, hinted to Palmerston in an interview that the Confederacy was prepared to do anything necessary if there was "some operating influence"—meaning the continuation of slavery—"that deterred Her Majesty's Government from recognizing us." Mason reported that Palmerston understood his message but that the prime minister did not take the bait. Rather, Palmerston simply noted that British recognition would do the Confederacy more harm than good because it would likely only anger the North and cause the Union to step up its military efforts. Ironically, the offer may have lacked substance anyway. In a private letter dated 22 March, Davis admitted that the Confederate government had no authority to bind its member states to an emancipation policy and that there was no guarantee that such a policy would ever secure approval at the state level.[18]

The disintegration of the Confederate government and the surrender of Confederate armies in April, May, and June 1865 brought Civil War diplomacy to its close. But the Civil War had a residual effect on U.S. foreign relations that survived the end of the fighting.

Diplomatic complications deriving from wartime European challenges to the Monroe Doctrine persisted after Appomattox. By that time, revolutionary forces had succeeded in overthrowing Spanish rule in the Dominican Republic. Spanish troops completed their evacuation of that country in July 1865.[19] However, the French proved tenacious in Mexico, resisting pressure from Seward, who remained as secretary of state under President Andrew Johnson, Lincoln's successor. When some high-ranking Confederate officers, including generals Edmund Kirby Smith, Jubal Early, and Joseph O. Shelby, participated in a mini-Confederate exodus to Mexico, fears mounted above the Mason-Dixon line that the South might one day use Mexico as a base to revive the Confederacy. In May 1865, Union general-in-chief Ulysses S. Grant posted General Philip H. Sheridan with an "army of occupation" on the Rio Grande to prevent southerners from reaching Mexico and to increase the pressure on Maximilian and the French. Sheridan came close to invading Mexico on the pretext of U.S.

claims to Confederate artillery pieces in the hands of Maximilian's forces at Matamoros, but Maximilian had the field pieces turned over to the United States rather than risk war. Finally, in February 1866, Napoleon announced a phased withdrawal from Mexico. The last French troops left the country in March 1867. Maximilian stayed on, only to suffer capture on 15 May by forces loyal to Benito Juárez, Mexican president before the French intervention. A Mexican firing squad executed Maximilian on 19 June 1867.[20]

Similarly, Civil War–related issues plagued U.S. relations with Great Britain well into the Reconstruction years. Following the war, the United States pressed claims against the British government for allegedly unneutral behavior during the conflict—including her allowing the raid on St. Albans to be launched from Canadian territory, but most especially her failure to prevent cruisers built in England for the Confederacy from leaving British ports. Britain, meanwhile, had its own claims against the United States government for damages incurred during the Civil War. It was not until September 1872 that an international tribunal of arbitration brought the most serious of these disputes, the *"Alabama* claims" concerning British shipbuilding for the Confederacy, to an end by awarding a $15,500,000 indemnity in gold to the United States, for damages committed by the *Florida, Alabama,* and the *Shenandoah.* The next year, a separate claims commission disallowed other U.S. claims against Britain but accorded Britain a $1,929,819 indemnity in gold for losses to British citizens.[21] Resolution of the claims controversy brought to a quietus the most significant diplomatic aftershock of the Civil War.

How are we to account for the Confederacy's diplomatic defeat? Were Lincoln, Seward, and Union diplomats in Europe and Latin America shrewder or more experienced in foreign relations than their Confederate counterparts? Or are there alternative explanations for the Union's triumphs on the diplomatic front?

Historians, in fact, generally credit Lincoln, Seward, and northern diplomats abroad, such as Adams in Britain and Thomas Corwin in Mexico, with superior skills in foreign relations. They by no means whitewash

Union diplomacy, for they report errors by Union diplomats, especially Seward. Many books and articles portray Seward as something of a loose cannon during his early tenure in the State Department. For instance, in an 1 April 1861 memorandum to Lincoln that reacted to Spanish and French interventionism in the Western Hemisphere as well as other matters, Seward recommended that Lincoln "demand explanations from *Spain* and *France,* categorically, at once," and then "convene Congress and declare war against them" unless "satisfactory explanations" were forthcoming. Less than two months later, in a draft communiqué to Adams, Seward rattled sabres against Great Britain. However, most scholars of Civil War diplomacy believe that Seward matured quickly as a diplomat, and Norman Ferris even argues that Seward played the calculating diplomat from the start. Seward, Ferris contends, always knew what he was about.[22]

Conversely, historians censure Confederate diplomats, though they make allowances for some of them, especially Benjamin and Slidell, and concede that Confederate diplomacy became more sophisticated over time in both its choice of personnel and its manipulation of foreign public opinion through propaganda. Historians chide Davis and his secretaries of state for choosing envoys who lacked the language competency essential for their positions, had previous political records that handicapped their missions, or suffered from personality flaws that made them "inappropriate," "inept," or "unfortunate" selections. How naive Davis must have been when, in 1861, he chose John T. Pickett as envoy to Mexico, a country that had been invaded by private military expeditions—filibusters—from California and Texas in the 1850s. Pickett, a fervent territorial expansionist who at one point during his mission warned the Mexican government that it could expect to be invaded by 30,000 Confederates if it allowed Union troops to cross its soil to contest Confederate claims to Arizona, had himself participated in a filibuster to Cuba. But the diplomatic blunders of Davis and his secretaries of state transcended their selections for foreign missions. Some dispatches emanating from the Confederate Department of State display a staggering insensitivity to foreign cultures. Perhaps the classic such document is a letter from Robert Toombs, the initial Confederate secretary of state, to Pickett, in which Toombs suggested

Pickett should curry favor with Mexicans by emphasizing the similarity between southern slavery and Mexican peonage. Since the Mexican Liberals ruling Mexico before the French intervention opposed peonage, these were bizarre instructions indeed![23]

Although there does not seem to be any obvious reason why Confederates should have made inferior diplomats, historians such as Allan Nevins and Emory M. Thomas have suggested that Confederates were bound to fail in foreign relations because they were much more provincial than northerners. They grew up in relatively rural surroundings and rarely traveled abroad or talked to foreigners. They simply did not understand foreign economies. Harboring "antique assumptions" about diplomacy, they could not comprehend how European foreign policy over the last century had come increasingly to be governed by considerations of realpolitik. Southerners, in other words, were simply less savvy than Yanks when it came to matters of the world.[24]

Few if any historians, however, would reduce the Union's diplomatic triumph to mere biographical determinism. Clearly other influences, including ideology, helped mold the responses of foreign governments to the American war. Confederate diplomats, in their search for recognition and aid, cited the basic principle of the Declaration of Independence that peoples have the right to alter their forms of government when their governments become oppressive. They assumed that foreign leaders and peoples already sympathizing with ongoing nationalistic movements on the European Continent would naturally gravitate to the Confederate cause. Thus Secretary of State Toombs, reacting to the unification of the Italian states and the proclamation of the Kingdom of Italy in March 1861, reasoned, "The recent course which the British Government pursued in relation to the recognition of the right of the Italian people to change their form of government and choose their own rulers encourages this Government to hope that they will pursue a similar policy in regard to the Confederate States." Historians confirm that this Confederate emphasis on the right of national self-determination carried weight abroad, even if it did not carry the day. To some degree, the 22 January 1863 Warsaw uprising against Russian rule over the Kingdom of Poland helped Confederate propagandists make this point. The resistance, which expanded into a widespread but ultimately repressed insurrection, attracted considerable sympathy in other countries, particularly France and Britain. Southern sympathizers in France, one study noted, drew parallels between the Confederacy's struggle against Lincoln and the resistance of Poles to Russia's tsar.[25]

Unfortunately for their missions, Confederate diplomats were hampered by their society's identification with slavery. In 1833, Great Britain's Parliament had abolished slavery throughout the empire as of 1 August 1834. Moreover, throughout the nineteenth century, the British government used treaties and applications of naval power to crusade against the African slave trade. France had ended slavery in its colonies in 1848. Most Latin American countries had long since done away with the institution. Austria and Russia had abolished serfdom—the latter by virtue of Alexander II's decree issued in March 1861, shortly before the Civil War began. Human bondage went against the grain of what we today might call world opinion.

Slavery crippled Confederate diplomacy from the start, though during the war's early phases, the Union government could only partially capitalize on antislavery sentiment abroad. For a variety of reasons, including a need to project a conservative image in order to keep four slave states that had not seceded (Delaware, Maryland, Kentucky, and Missouri) in the Union, the Lincoln administration maintained for some time that the North's purpose in waging war was to restore the Union rather than to abolish slavery. Even Lincoln's Emancipation Proclamation (1 January 1863) did not entirely end slavery. Rather, it promised to end slavery in Confederate areas afterwards conquered by the Union army. Technically, therefore, slavery would continue in the four slave states still in the Union as well as in the new state of West Virginia (which entered the Union with provisions freeing persons born after 4 July 1863 but only gradually emancipating slaves born before that date) and Confederate areas already under Union occupation. It was the Thirteenth Amendment to the Constitution, passed by Congress on 31 January 1865—virtually at the war's end— rather than the Emancipation Proclamation, that ended slavery in North

America. Still, slavery disintegrated throughout the South as the war progressed. Union troops liberated slaves even in the slave states that had not seceded. Slaves ran away by the thousands to Union lines. Those who did not run away often refused to labor any longer for their masters. Foreign governments therefore came to understand that a Union victory would destroy slavery, and this awareness made matters ever more difficult for Confederate diplomats already engaged in an uphill struggle. Certainly Confederate diplomat A. Dudley Mann discovered this to be the case during his audience with Pope Pius IX in November 1863: "His Holiness . . . stated . . . that Lincoln and Company had endeavored to create an impression abroad that they were fighting for the abolition of slavery, and that it might perhaps be judicious in us to consent to gradual emancipation."[26] Slavery may not have been the primary determinant of foreign reactions to the American Civil War, but it put Confederate diplomats on the defensive throughout the conflict.

Although the Confederates expected economic forces to prompt foreign recognition and aid, some historians have advanced economic interpretations of why Union diplomacy prevailed. That is, historians have probed for flaws in the South's "king cotton" logic, such as its neglect of "king corn," to help clarify why Britain and other powers never intervened in the Civil War to rescue the Confederacy. In 1861, the United States supplied 44.7 percent of Great Britain's wheat, flour, and maize. Substantial northern grain shipments also found their way to Russia, Prussia, and France. Did northern grain neutralize southern cotton? Some historians believe this indeed to have been the case. (Others argue that Europeans knew that they could have found alternate supplies of wheat if necessary, and that corn thus never approximated cotton as a factor in European decision-making.) Scholars also note that investments in northern railroads and canals as well as links between northern and British financial houses gave the British people a vested interest in the Union cause that would be jeopardized if their government helped the Confederacy. Furthermore, windfall profits accruing to certain sectors of the British economy because of the Civil War helped to compensate for the damage the war caused to her cotton industry. Cotton shortages, for example, created more demand for British and French woolens and linens. The Civil War also proved to be a boon for British shipbuilders and their employees, as well as for European producers of small arms and other munitions who supplied both the Union and Confederate armies.[27]

Finally, historians recognize that affairs across the Atlantic played a significant and perhaps transcendent role in diverting European governments from involvement in the American Civil War. European intervention in the Civil War was unlikely to occur unless it came in the form of a joint Anglo-French intervention, possibly involving other powers; but the Anglo-French alliance that had fought Russia in the Crimean War just a few years earlier (1854–56) was very shaky by the time of the Civil War. British leaders did not entirely trust the government of Napoleon III, which had annexed Nice and Savoy in 1860 and confirmed its expansionist inclinations in Mexico after the outbreak of the American conflict.[28] Moreover, all of the major European powers had a stake in developments on the Continent that occurred while the American Civil War was in progress. France kept a garrison in Rome to protect the Papal State against the territorial ambitions of the new Italian kingdom. Britain, France, and Austria rendered diplomatic support to the Polish uprising of 1863, but Prussia sided with Russia in the crisis. In 1864, Austria and Prussia went to war with Denmark in response to Denmark's annexation of the duchy of Schleswig the previous year, but relations between Austria and Prussia were already so strained that those states would be at war with each other two years later. Britain and France participated in diplomatic initiatives designed to end the Austro-Prussian war against Denmark.

Conflict on the Continent indirectly touched North America when Russia sent naval squadrons to New York and San Francisco in late 1863 because of the European crisis over Poland. Should war break out with Britain, Russian leaders reasoned, their ships would be safe from the superior British navy in neutral American ports. Misinterpreting Russian purposes, northerners celebrated what seemed to them a gesture of Russian solidarity with the Union cause.[29]

More frequently, Continental matters drew the attention of European policymakers away from the North American war. William L. Dayton, the

Union's minister to France, explained on one occasion, "The insurrection of Poland has driven American affairs out of view for the moment." Foreign leaders realized that intervention in the Civil War would limit their ability to react to rapidly unfolding events on the Continent and alterations in the European balance of power. Such considerations doubly affected Napoleon III, who was already militarily embroiled in Mexico and on the European Continent. The result, as D. P. Crook put it, was that "the distractions of European power politics helped materially to save the Union."[30] Perhaps, we might add, Confederates never really controlled their own diplomatic destiny.

In the following essays, Howard Jones, R. J. M. Blackett, Thomas Schoonover, and James M. McPherson probe and illuminate Civil War diplomacy. Their pieces help us to better understand not only why Confederate diplomacy came to such a sorry end but also the meaning of the Civil War to the international community and the war's place within the overall story of nineteenth-century world history.

Jones's essay reconsiders what may well be the Civil War diplomatic question that has most intrigued historians: What kept Great Britain from recognizing the Confederacy or otherwise intervening in the conflict? Since Napoleon III made it clear that France would become involved in the war only in conjunction with British intervention, Britain held the key to Confederate diplomatic hopes.

Utilizing exhaustive research in British archival sources, Jones provides a step-by-step account of British decision-making during one of the Civil War's diplomatic turning points: the period in late 1862 when the British government seriously considered trying, in combination with France and Russia, to mediate an end to the fighting. Jones explains that had this attempt been made, it might have culminated in British recognition of the Confederacy and an Anglo-Union war, and uncovers the role of British secretary for war George Cornewall Lewis in defeating the initiative. Jones's essay is particularly interesting because it argues, in contradiction of numerous other accounts, that the Union victory at Antietam and Lincoln's Emancipation Proclamation in many ways heightened, rather than dampened, European interest in intervention. Jones also makes the case that British leaders were so shocked by the Civil War's bloodshed that humanitarian principles fed their interest in mediating an end to the war, even if their reactions to the war were primarily shaped by principles of national self-interest.

R. J. M. Blackett also treats British diplomacy in his essay, but from an entirely different perspective. Whereas Jones's essay is traditional in the sense that it deals with policy-making at the highest political levels, Blackett's piece represents the new social history, with its insistence that scholars study the past from the "bottom up"—that is, from the perspective of society's underclasses. For Blackett, these underclasses are former southern slaves who gave anti-Confederate public lectures in Britain during the Civil War and the thousands of workers in Britain's cotton district who attended meetings to consider British policy regarding the conflict in the United States. He argues that even though there is no evidence that British policy toward the Civil War would have been different had public opinion taken a different course, it was then an "almost universally accepted conviction that government policy was susceptible to public pressure." Drawing from accounts in British newspapers and other documents, Blackett shows that pro–Union African American orators played a key role in neutralizing efforts by Confederate propaganda agents and British sympathizers of the South to convey an image that British textile workers favored intervention on behalf of the South. For southern sympathizers to have any chance of manipulating British policy by use of public opinion, they needed to project an image of a working-class consensus in favor of recognition of the Confederacy. Instead, the best that they could deliver was evidence that textile workers were divided on the American war.

Thomas Schoonover's essay provides a striking contrast to those of Jones and Blackett. Schoonover frames his piece with the world-systems theory of Immanuel Wallerstein. He also considers Civil War diplomacy from an unusually generous chronological and geographical perspective. In fact, Schoonover chides U.S. historians collectively for their narrow perspective regarding Civil War diplomacy.

Schoonover's primary contention is that before, during, and after the Civil War, Americans and Europeans competed diplomatically, economically, culturally, and sometimes militarily for advantages in the countries of the Gulf-Caribbean region, often for purposes of social imperialism (improving conditions at home through expansionist and other initiatives abroad). Historians who do not relate Civil War–era developments to this long-standing competition, Schoonover believes, misread their meaning. Schoonover argues that the Union was better situated than the Confederacy for this multinational confrontation because of its superior prewar economic position. He gives particular emphasis to the French intervention in Mexico, which he implies would likely have happened even had the Civil War not been in progress, but also pays attention to a variety of European initiatives involving Spain, Prussia, and other countries. Schoonover's essay fits Union schemes to colonize American blacks in the Gulf-Caribbean area within his social imperialism construct and shows how Union diplomats tried to stave off the French through loans to Mexico's government. He argues that the Confederacy, which surprisingly assigned about half its diplomatic agents to the region, nevertheless made a poor diplomatic showing there. Instead of pursuing commercial advantages in the Gulf-Caribbean, Confederate planners put too much emphasis upon ineffective plots to seize Union gold shipments moving through the area. Taken as a whole, Schoonover's essay not only covers a wide chunk of the Civil War's diplomatic history but also serves as a caution against any ethnocentric reading of the American past.

James M. McPherson's essay probes the meaning of the American Civil War to other peoples and governments, especially in Europe and Latin America. In contrast to Schoonover's piece, which in a sense downplays the Civil War's importance in the overall scheme of things, McPherson's essay tends to underline its significance in human history by arguing that peoples in other countries carefully followed the Civil War and were profoundly affected by its outcome. "[L]iberals, radicals, progressives, reformers, and revolutionaries" everywhere drew inspiration from the United States before the war. While the war was in progress, they tended, especially after the abolition of slavery was incorporated into Union war aims, to accept the war on Lincoln's terms, to view the Union as the embodiment of democracy and of the hopes of oppressed peoples everywhere. In contrast, conservative elites in other countries tended to disparage American democracy, welcomed the breakup of the Union, and often supported the Confederacy. McPherson suggests a bit less tentatively than Blackett, though he hedges his argument with qualifiers, that public opinion may have kept the British and French governments from recognizing or otherwise helping the Confederacy. McPherson gives attention to Russia's role in the Civil War and provides a brief but revealing look at Russian minister to the United States Edouard de Stoeckl's reactions to the war—which exposed a number of the crosscurrents of world opinion about what was happening in North America. McPherson explains that the Union's victory gave renewed inspiration to liberals abroad, including supporters of expanded suffrage in Britain, republicans in Spain, and abolitionists in Brazil and Cuba.

Allan Nevins once mused that the "future of the world as we know it" rode on the outcome of Civil War diplomacy; had Great Britain intervened on the Confederate side, it might well have led to the Union's conquest of Canada and France's retention of Mexico and probably would have ruled out the Anglo-American coalitions that helped win World War I and defeat Hitler in World War II. "No battle," Nevins declared, "not Gettysburg, not the Wilderness, was more important than the contest waged in the diplomatic arena and the forum of public opinion."[31] One need not agree with Nevins's speculations to grasp his point. Americans will never truly comprehend their Civil War until they claim its diplomatic front. There are no Civil War diplomatic history museums to parallel the many battlefield parks that perpetuate memories of the war's generals, soldiers, campaigns, and battles in the American mind. Perhaps there should be. These four essays remind us that we have much to learn about how foreign nations affected the course of the war, and how the course of the war affected the peoples and governments of other countries.

NOTES

1. Alfred Jackson Hanna and Kathryn Abbey Hanna, *Napoleon III and Mexico: American Triumph over Monarchy* (Chapel Hill, 1971), 185; James W. Cortada, *Spain and the American Civil War: Relations at Mid-Century, 1855–1868, Transactions of the American Philosophical Society,* vol. 70, pt. 4 (Philadelphia, 1950), 30–35. Though Spanish troops landed in Santo Domingo months earlier, the reannexation was only consummated upon Queen Isabella's issuing a formal decree to that end on 19 May.

A Spanish admiral seized the Chincha Islands from Peru during the Civil War (in 1864), but the seizure was prompted by Spanish demands for redress regarding the death of a Spaniard and injuries to other Spanish emigrants in an incident in Peru in 1863, rather than from any long-term expansionist scheme. In this instance, the Union government did offer to mediate the dispute. Cortada, *Spain and the American Civil War,* 94–101.

2. Jay Luvaas, *The Military Legacy of the Civil War: The European Inheritance* (Chicago, 1959), 2, 5–9, 21, and passim; Arthur J. L. Fremantle, *Three Months in the Southern States, April–June 1863* (Edinburgh, 1863).

3. Confederate diplomats waited until January 1863 to formally press their demand for recognition on King Leopold II's Belgian government. See A. Dudley Mann to Judah P. Benjamin, 5 January 1863, with enclosure, in James D. Richardson, ed. and comp., *The Messages and Papers of Jefferson Davis and the Confederacy, Including Diplomatic Correspondence, 1861–1865,* 2 vols. (1905; reprint, New York, 1966), 2:385–89 [hereafter cited as *Messages*].

4. William Morrison Robinson, Jr., *The Confederate Privateers* (New Haven, 1928), 1–24; Howard Jones, *Union in Peril: The Crisis over British Intervention in the Civil War* (Chapel Hill, 1992), 38–42. For the stipulations of the Confederate privateering legislation, which were generous regarding the percentage of the value of prizes that privateers could retain for their own profit and which exempted slaveholding states and territories still in the Union, see Robinson, *Confederate Privateers,* 18–24.

5. Frank L. Owsley, *King Cotton Diplomacy* (Chicago, 1931), 1–24.

6. *Congressional Globe,* 35 Cong., 1 Sess., Appendix, 70; William Howard Russell, *My Diary North and South,* ed. Eugene H. Berwanger (New York, 1988), 82.

7. W. L. Yancey and A. Dudley Mann to Robert Toombs, 21 May, 1 June, 15 July 1861, in *Messages,* 2:34–38; Mary Chesnut Diary, 5 August 1861, in C. Vann Woodward and Elisabeth Muhlenfeld, eds., *The Private Mary Chesnut: The Unpublished Civil War Diaries* (New York, 1984), 116.

8. Jones, *Union in Peril,* 34, 68, 155; J. G. Randall and David Donald, *The Civil War and Reconstruction,* 2d ed. (Boston, 1966), 287; Donaldson Jordan and Edwin J. Pratt, *Europe and the American Civil War* (New York, 1969), 197–98; Serge Gavronsky, *The French Liberal Opposition and the American Civil War* (New York, 1968), 118–23; Mary Ellison, *Support for Secession: Lancashire and the American Civil War* (Chicago, 1972).

9. D. P. Crook, *Diplomacy during the American Civil War* (New York, 1975), 43–44; Jones, *Union in Peril,* 80–81; Frank J. Merli, *Great Britain and the Confederate Navy, 1861–1865* (Bloomington, 1970), 74–85. For book-length studies of the *Trent* incident, see Norman Ferris, *The Trent Affair: A Diplomatic Crisis* (Knoxville, 1977); and Gordon H. Warren, *Fountain of Discontent: The Trent Affair and Freedom of the Seas* (Boston, 1981).

10. Daniel B. Carroll, *Henri Mercier and the American Civil War* (Princeton, 1971), 97–118; Crook, *Diplomacy,* 44–60; Jones, *Union in Peril,* 83–99; Robin W. Winks, *Canada and the United States: The Civil War Years* (Baltimore, 1960), 69–103.

11. Winks, *Canada and the United States,* x, 67, 295–333, 337–41; Dennis K. Wilson, *Justice under Pressure: The Saint Albans Raid and Its Aftermath* (Lanham, Md., 1992). Young and four of his followers were rearrested on December 20. They were tried for robbery, but the judge quashed the charges. Later they were rearrested on charges of violating British neutrality. But Young was released in October 1865.

12. Mark E. Neely, Jr., *The Fate of Liberty: Abraham Lincoln and Civil Liberties* (New York, 1991), 25, 141–43. Most British sailors captured for running the blockade were released after a short while.

13. William M. Browne to William L. Yancey, Pierre A. Rost, and A. Dudley Mann, 29 April 1861, in *Messages,* 2:19; Richard I. Lester, *Confederate Finance and Purchasing in Great Britain* (Charlottesville, 1975), viii, 10–22, 133–94; Hanna and Hanna, *Napoleon III and Mexico,* 155–64. The Confederacy's most ambitious borrowing scheme occurred in 1863, when Slidell and Huse arranged that French financier Emile Erlanger underwrite the sale of Confederate cotton bonds. Estimates on how much money this arrangement netted the Confederacy vary from less than $3 million to more than $8 million. See the discussion in Clement Eaton, *Jefferson Davis* (New York, 1977), 198. For a study downplaying the significance of purchases abroad in the Confederate military effort on the grounds that Confederate domestic production of munitions was far more significant, see Richard E. Beringer et al., *Why the South Lost the Civil War* (Athens, Ga., 1986), 53–63.

14. Warren F. Spencer, *The Confederate Navy in Europe* (University, Ala., 1983), 38–92; Lester, *Confederate Finance,* 61–114; Lynn M. Case and Warren F. Spencer, *The United States and France: Civil War Diplomacy* (Philadelphia, 1970), 430, 433.

15. Judah P. Benjamin to Henry Hotze, 5 September 1863, in *Messages,* 2:562; Phillip Thomas Tucker, *The Confederacy's Fighting Chaplain: Father John B. Bannon* (Tuscaloosa, 1992); Hanna and Hanna, *Napoleon III and Mexico,* 160–61. Vidaurri, whose control extended over much of northeastern Mexico, including Matamoros, had his own agenda in suggesting the alliance. Vidaurri wanted to carve out his own republic within northern Mexico with Confederate help. The Davis administration did not agree to the alliance.

16. Benjamin to Mason, 4 August 1863; Lord Russell to Slidell, Mason, and Mann, 25 November 1864; Benjamin to Slidell, 20 September 1864; Slidell to Benjamin, 17 November 1864, in *Messages,* 2:540, 687, 677, 684; Case and Spencer, *United States*

and France, 427–80. Eventually the British government purchased the Laird rams for the Royal Navy. Most of the purchase price was refunded to the Confederacy. Merli, *Great Britain and the Confederate Navy,* 195–212.

17. Benjamin to Henry Hotze, 5 September 1863; Benjamin to Mason, 4 August 1863; Lord Russell to Slidell, Mason, and Mann, 25 November 1864; Benjamin to Lucius Q. C. Lamar, 19 November 1862, 11 June 1863, in *Messages,* 2:562–63, 364–68, 505–506; James B. Murphy, *L. Q. C. Lamar: Pragmatic Patriot* (Baton Rouge, 1973), 72–77

18. Cleburne to Johnston, 2 January 1864; Davis to J. D. Shaw, 22 March 1865, in Robert F. Durden, *The Gray and the Black: The Confederate Debate on Emancipation* (Baton Rouge, 1972), 54–62, 266–67; Mason to Benjamin, 31 March 1865, with enclosures, in *Messages,* 2:709–19; Eli N. Evans, *Judah P. Benjamin: The Jewish Confederate* (New York, 1988), 262–64, 268, 275, 278–79.

19. Rayford W. Logan, *Haiti and the Dominican Republic* (New York, 1968), 40–42; Samuel Flagg Bemis, *The Latin American Policy of the United States: An Historical Interpretation* (New York, 1943), 112–13.

20. Crook, *Diplomacy,* 171–84; Andrew F. Rolle, *The Lost Cause: The Confederate Exodus to Mexico* (Norman, Okla., 1965), 3–4, 21–25, 37, 53–56, 80n; Hanna and Hanna, *Napoleon III and Mexico,* 221–35; Thomas Schoonover, *Dollars over Dominion: The Triumph of Liberalism in Mexican-United States Relations, 1861–1867* (Baton Rouge, 1978); Roy Morris, *Sheridan: The Life and Wars of General Phil Sheridan* (New York, 1992), 260–65. Estimates of Confederate exiles in Mexico between 1865 and 1867 range from 1,000–4,000 people.

21. Randall and Donald, *Civil War and Reconstruction,* 671–77; Adrian Cook, *The Alabama Claims: American Politics and Anglo-American Relations, 1865–1872* (Ithaca, N.Y., 1975), 238–39; Alexander DeConde, *A History of American Foreign Policy,* 2d. ed. (New York, 1973), 280–84; Winks, *Canada and the United States,* 333.

22. Allan Nevins, *The War for the Union,* 4 vols. (New York, 1959–71), 1:61, 2:242–74, 3:473–513; Norman B. Ferris, *Desperate Diplomacy: William H. Seward's Foreign Policy, 1861* (Knoxville, 1976), vii, 3–4, 6–13, 55, 60–62, 91–92, 180–82, 195–96, 200, 203–5; Stephen B. Oates, *With Malice toward None: The Life of Abraham Lincoln* (New York, 1977), 241–45, 271–72, 340; Winks, *Canada and the United States,* 22–51, 319; Glyndon G. Van Deusen, *William Henry Seward* (New York, 1967), 280–84, 292–323, 349–75; Martin B. Duberman, *Charles Francis Adams, 1807–1886* (Boston, 1961), 258–322. Most scholars contend that Seward's 1 April memorandum was designed to reunify the United States by means of a foreign war in defense of the Monroe Doctrine. Allan Nevins, however, refines this argument by suggesting that Seward contemplated a war against Spain in which the United States would try to conquer Cuba. Since the slave island had long been an objective of southern expansionists, southerners would never have allowed the North to conquer it alone. Nevins further contends that Seward believed that Cuba would provide a base for Union military operations

against the Confederacy in the event that a U.S.-Spanish war did not produce reunion. Nevins, *War for the Union*, 1:62–63.

23. Clement Eaton, *Jefferson Davis* (New York, 1977), 164–73; Charles P. Roland, *The Confederacy* (Chicago, 1960), 100–124; Evans, *Judah P. Benjamin*, 156–291; Hanna and Hanna, *Napoleon III and Mexico*, 51–53; Emory M. Thomas, *The Confederate Nation, 1861–1865* (New York, 1979), 167–89; William C. Davis, *Jefferson Davis: The Man and His Hour* (New York, 1991), 384–86; Schoonover, *Dollars over Dominion*, 9, 38; Toombs to Pickett with enclosure of "Memorandum of Instructions," 17 May 1861, in *Messages*, 2:20–26.

24. Nevins, *War for the Union*, 1:97; Thomas, *Confederate Nation*, 138, 139, 167–71.

25. Toombs to William L. Yancey, Pierre A. Rost, and A. Dudley Mann, 16 March 1861; Yancey and Mann to Toombs, 15 July 1861, in *Messages*, 2:3–8, 42–46; Nevins, *War for the Union*, 2:252; Jones, *Union in Peril*, 22; Gavronsky, *French Liberal Opposition*, 159.

26. Mann to Benjamin, 14 November 1863, in *Messages*, 2:591–95.

27. Owsley, *King Cotton Diplomacy*, 567–77; Crook, *Diplomacy*, 11–12, 109–110; Randall and Donald, *Civil War and Reconstruction*, 503–4; Case and Spencer, *United States and France*, 379.

28. Jones, *Union in Peril*, 72–73; Crook, *Diplomacy*, 7, 37–38.

29. William Appleman Williams, *American-Russian Relations, 1781–1947* (New York, 1971), 20; Crook, *Diplomacy*, 145–46.

30. Case and Spencer, *United States and France*, 1, 351, 398–99, 400 (quotation); Crook, *Diplomacy*, 124, 185–86; Carroll, *Henri Mercier*, 315–19.

31. Nevins, *War for the Union*, 2:242.

HISTORY AND MYTHOLOGY

The Crisis over British Intervention in the Civil War

★ ★ ★

HOWARD JONES

*I*n late 1862, the British government attempted to mastermind a European intervention in the American Civil War that would doubt-less have assured southern independence. To date, historians have not adequately explained why that intervention never took place, though there is substantial agreement that a European involvement in the war would have had momentous consequences for the North, the South, and the European powers. If only the British had intervened in the Civil War, so say the most ardent proponents of the "Lost Cause," the Confederate States of America would have won independence and taken its rightful place among the community of nations. Such a dramatic move by En-gland, they insist, would have encouraged France and other nations on the Continent to do the same. Diplomatic recognition of the Confederacy would have dealt the Union a devastating blow, for the monumental step would have undermined the Constitution by justifying secession and thereby safeguarded slavery and the entire southern way of life.

According to conventional accounts, the Battle of Antietam in Sep-tember 1862 marked a major turning point in the war because it led to the Emancipation Proclamation and thereby blocked British intervention on the side of the slaveholding South. Pulitzer Prize–winning historian James M. McPherson insists that the battle "frustrated Confederate hopes for British recognition and precipitated the Emancipation Proclamation. . . . Thus ended the South's best chance for European intervention." Stephen W. Sears largely agrees: "If Antietam abruptly halted the movement toward foreign intervention, the proclamation on emancipation put the seal on the matter." And Frank L. Owsley declared that Antietam marked "the death-blow of Confederate recognition," for British prime minister Lord Palmerston "turned against present mediation when the news of Confederate military failure arrived."[1]

GEORGE CORNEWALL LEWIS
(from Gilbert F. Lewis, ed., Letters of George Cornewall Lewis)

Mythology has often taken the place of history, and nowhere is this more so than in the Union's crisis over British intervention in the Civil War. Contrary to the long-accepted view stated above, the truth is that these pivotal events of autumn 1862 actually *heightened* British interest in intervention. The reason is clear: the interventionists, led by Foreign Secretary Lord John Russell and Chancellor of the Exchequer William E. Gladstone, feared that emancipation would incite a wave of slave revolts that would grow into a race war and, combined with the escalating hostilities between North and South, ultimately pull England and other nations into the fiery conflict. As the intervention crisis built, however, a less-known figure assumed statesmanlike status. Secretary for War George Cornewall Lewis emerged as the chief opposition leader to a British involvement that probably would have led to war between England and the Union.[2]

Americans have little understanding of the important international repercussions of the battle for Fort Sumter. Indeed, the focus on America's domestic crisis after April 1861 has distorted the history of this era by sharply diminishing the role of diplomacy. Both from television—especially from the widely acclaimed PBS series by Ken Burns—and the numerous books on the military aspects of the war, one gains the impression that President Abraham Lincoln successfully defined this struggle as totally domestic in nature. Appearances belie reality. The president did not succeed in keeping the distinction clear between a rebellion and a war, and the result was that foreign and domestic problems meshed. The Lincoln administration's greatest fear in foreign affairs was that England would extend diplomatic recognition to the Confederacy. Of all instructions to the Union's minister in England, Charles Francis Adams, the only one directing him to suspend his functions as a diplomat would follow a British announcement of recognition. Whether British intervention took the form of a mediation, an armistice, or recognition itself, the White House had to block such an involvement—even by threatening war.[3]

England intended its official position of neutrality to keep its people out of the war while permitting trade with both North and South. But given England's strategic positions in Canada and the West Indies, along with its growing commercial interests in the Atlantic, trouble was certain. From the beginning of the American conflict, the Palmerston ministry expressed concern over the Union's dissolution, whether or not secession was legal. The prime minister, ever pragmatic and realistic, voiced the sentiment of many in his country by insisting that southern separation was a *fait accompli*—especially after the Union army's disaster at Bull Run in the summer of 1861—and often lamented the North's stubborn unwillingness to make that admission. Russell, Palmerston's diminutive but headstrong foreign secretary, agonized over the trial of the Union and the harmful economic impact it had on England, and came to consider southern independence a fair price to pay for peace. For humanitarian as well as economic reasons, he joined Gladstone in calling for an intervention intended to end the war. As for slavery, Russell and others

LORD JOHN RUSSELL (courtesy Massachusetts Historical Society)

in England proposed a remedy: "One Republic to be constituted on the principle of freedom & personal liberty—the other on the principle of slavery & the mutual surrender of fugitives."[4]

Whether these British spokesmen believed their own humanitarian pronouncements remains difficult to determine; but they lived in the Victorian Age in England, when expressions of concern for others—including Americans on both sides of the conflict—were not uncommon from all levels of British society. The great majority of British interventionists were not so malevolent as to want the American republic to commit national suicide so they might further their own ends; they wanted to stop the war for humanity in general and for British textile workers in particular. Of course, some Britons saw military, economic, and strategic advantages resulting from a dismembered United States. And, of course, British humanitarian concerns did not exist in a vacuum; peace in America would revive commerce as well as stop a war that threatened to destroy both antagonists and, in the process, pull in outside nations. Again and again, Russell offered assurances of sympathy for the Union; repeatedly he stressed the inhumanity of continuing a war that had demonstrated the hopelessness of reunion. Yet even if he was moved more by economic than humanitarian concerns, the two interests were not incompatible. Time was the key consideration: the American war threatened to inflict great economic hardships on England—particularly once its cotton surplus ran out by the end of 1862. But any form of intervention would necessarily challenge the Union blockade, and everyone knew it would constitute an act of war.[5]

The British minister in Washington, Lord Lyons, realized the dangers in intervention. He had warned early in the war that for recognition to bring an end to the fighting, the intervening powers must be prepared to use military force because the North would most likely refuse to lay down its arms. Recognition would not end the war unless the intervening powers negotiated "a defensive (if not an offensive) Alliance with the South." But such a pact, Lyons warned, would lead to war with the Union.[6]

Even though the British had several reasons for intervention, their most serious concern was the horror of the war, which was accentuated by a fear of slave insurrections in the South that would develop into a race war of national proportions. To the House of Lords in early 1862, Russell expressed his anxieties over this dire possibility. Numerous British observers dreaded the outbreak of servile war; not only would such an event disrupt the cotton economy for years, but a racial upheaval would rock the South and perhaps the entire republic once the chains of bondage were broken. Indeed, such a calamity could upset the entire commercial relationship with the United States—including the British importation of northern wheat. Yet this very crisis seemed to be developing almost in conjunction with the waning hopes of the Lincoln administration. As early as January 1862, in the midst of the *Trent* war scare with England, Lyons alerted Russell that the American conflict was "rapidly tending towards the issue either of peace and a recognition of the separation, or a Proclamation of Emancipation and the raising of a servile insurrection." Russell was alarmed that the president should want "a war of emancipation." Yet out of desperation, the foreign secretary and others believed, Lincoln might instigate a servile war once he realized that he could not restore the Union by other means.[7]

By the spring of 1862, the White House seemed prepared to take that momentous step. To counter the threat of intervention, Secretary of State William H. Seward inadvertently provided substance for England's deepest fear: he warned the London government that its involvement in American affairs could set off a slave revolt that would spawn a race war in the United States. In a dispatch meant for Russell's perusal, Seward wrote Adams that before the fall of New Orleans to Union forces that previous April, Europe had speculated about an intervention that could only have benefited the South. Now, despite the Union victory, British interest in such a scheme had not abated. An intervention based on southern separation would guarantee a servile war disruptive to the economy and injurious to all European interests in America.[8]

The British became instantly alarmed by the ensuing events of the summer. In late July, the chargé in Washington, William Stuart, reported that the Union had shifted its wartime objective to antislavery. He was correct. Lincoln had recently informed his cabinet of this decision, although agreeing with Seward to delay a public announcement until there was news of a northern victory on the battlefield. Otherwise, England might interpret emancipation as a last-ditch effort to win the war. To undercut the South, Stuart feared, the North seemed ready to instigate a slave uprising intended to break the back of the Confederate army by forcing its soldiers to return home to protect their families. These developments, along with Seward's warning regarding slave insurrections, deeply troubled Russell. Indeed, in his anxiety he misinterpreted Seward's note to mean that the Lincoln administration was prepared to stir up a slave rebellion in a desperate effort to ward off foreign intervention. So serious were Russell's fears that Stuart read Russell's dispatch to Seward and later gave him a copy to drive home the point. The possibility of a race war, Russell insisted, would "only make other nations more desirous to see an end of this desolating and destructive conflict."[9]

The Union's move against slavery so repelled the British that it encouraged the very intervention that the Lincoln administration sought to prevent. Most British observers did not believe that the Union advanced emancipation as a moral and humanitarian measure. When the war began, they had been surprised when the White House emphasized that the conflict did not concern slavery. They failed to understand, as Lincoln did, that a war against slavery would alienate slaveowners in the loyal border states, as well as Unionists in the Confederacy, and that few northern males were prepared to fight a war on behalf of blacks. Even if Lincoln had legitimate concerns about the domestic political consequences of a war against slavery, the British complained that he took the side of his countrymen—including those outside the Republican Party as well as those within—who had condoned slavery by refusing to take a stand against it. The British now regarded emancipation as hypocrisy—a desperate effort to save the Union by encouraging the South's slaves to rebel and bring down the Cotton Kingdom from within. The only remedy to this demonic action, from England's perspective, was an intervention premised on southern separation.

The Lincoln administration became infuriated with the British. The "slaveholding insurgents," Seward disgustedly told Adams, had asked other nations to help overthrow the American government, and then, in an effort to safeguard slavery, they stabbed those same nations in the back by blocking the cotton flow. The South's actions were not only treason against the Union but a war against humanity. How could England fail to grasp these truths? Nothing the Union did, Seward bitterly complained, had a favorable impact on Europe. Victory "does not satisfy our enemies abroad. Defeats in their eyes prove our national incapacity." And now the Union's stand against slavery had failed to arouse support, even in England. "At first the [Union] government was considered as unfaithful to humanity in not proclaiming emancipation, and when it appeared that slavery, by being thus forced into the contest, must suffer, and perhaps perish in the conflict, then the war had become an intolerable propagandism of emancipation by the sword." If other nations intervened, Seward darkly warned, the American conflict would become "a war of the world."[10]

The Union and British governments had taken different roads that led to the same destination. Each was convinced that the other's policies assured a war of atrocity that could become racial in the United States before it became international. As the Union warned that intervention would prolong the war, raise the tempo of the fighting, and ultimately spread the conflict beyond America's boundaries, so did the British come to believe that failure to intervene—and soon—would guarantee the same results.

European mediation—and perhaps recognition—seemed imminent in mid-September 1862, when news arrived in London of another resounding Union defeat—again at Bull Run. The British must have experienced a feeling of *déjà vu* upon receiving word of the second major engagement at Bull Run. At long last, the Union stood on the brink of a convincing defeat that would force it to give up the ill-conceived attempt to subjugate the South. And how bittersweet that fate had cast its judgment for northern humiliation again at Bull Run. Surely, British observers noted with impatience, the Union would not tempt fate again. In France, Foreign Minister Edouard Thouvenel observed that no reasonable leader on the Continent thought the Union could win. But again European hopes turned into exasperation. In a reaction similar to that after First Bull Run, the Lincoln administration neither lost its resolve to win the war nor its resistance to intervention. Union spirits soared even as disaster threatened to follow a trail northward.[11]

To many British observers, the second Union defeat at Bull Run had underlined the North's inability to subjugate the South and therefore justified a move toward ending the war on the basis of a separation. In London the *Times* and the *Morning Post* (which both usually expressed Palmerston's views) leaned toward recognition, whereas the *Morning Herald* made a broader appeal: "Let us do something, as we are Christian men." Whether "arbitration, intervention, diplomatic action, recognition of the South, remonstrance with the North, friendly interference or forcible pressure of some sort . . . , let us do something to stop this carnage." Palmerston thought the time for intervention was nigh. "The federals . . . got a very complete smashing," he wrote Russell on 14 September, "and it seems not altogether unlikely that still greater disasters await them, and that even Washington or Baltimore may fall into the hands of the Confederates. If this should happen, would it not be time for us to consider whether . . . England and France might not address the contending parties and recommend an arrangement upon the basis of separation?" If the mediation offer were rejected, he insisted, "we ought ourselves to recognize the Southern States as an independent State."[12]

The South's second victory at Bull Run had started a move toward British intervention, a mediation based on a division of the United States and one, if rejected, to be followed by recognition. From the Union's perspective, of course, the distinction between mediation and recognition might well not have existed: either action would constitute interference in American domestic affairs and encourage the South to maintain its resistance. In all probability, mediation would serve as a practical prelude to recognition, assuring British acknowledgment of southern independence as an accomplished fact. But before the ministry could begin the diplomatic procedure leading to mediation, word arrived that General Robert E. Lee's Confederate forces had launched a daring raid into Maryland.

The move toward British intervention had approached a climactic point by the late summer of 1862. Indeed, if Lee had not followed his success at

Bull Run with an immediate march north, the South might have won a mediation followed by recognition. But the full impact of Second Bull Run had not yet settled on London when Lee decided to take the war into Maryland, inspiring hope among southern strategists of bringing about the intervention that, ironically, may have been already in their grasp.

Although both Palmerston and Russell had turned to mediation after Second Bull Run, the prime minister remained concerned about a Union refusal to cooperate. Consequently, the news of a southern advance northward made Palmerston hope that Lee might win again, thereby increasing the chances for Union acquiescence in a mediation. Another series of Confederate victories, particularly if they occurred in Union territory, might finally persuade the North to recognize the war's futility and accept peace. Palmerston seemed relieved as he wrote Russell on 22 September: "Though the time for making a communication

LORD PALMERSTON (courtesy Massachusetts Historical Society)

to the United States is evidently coming, yet perhaps it is partly actually come." The two armies were nearing each other north of Washington, and "another great conflict is about to take place." Since the "northern Fury has not as yet sufficiently spent itself," another sound defeat north of Washington might put its leaders into "a more reasonable state of mind." Russell concurred.[13]

Palmerston nonetheless saw great difficulties in mediation. Even if both North and South accepted the offer, a question would develop whether "the fact of our meddling would not of itself be tantamount to an acknowledgment of the Confederacy as an independent State." More explosive would be the ramifications of a mediation that the South accepted and the North did not. For at least that reason alone, Palmerston believed, England and France must invite the Union's friend, Russia, to participate. With Russia involved, the North would be more likely to go along. Even if the Russians declined, as he knew was probable, England would have won credibility with them by extending the invitation. Admittedly, it was better not to have the Russians' involvement because of their avowed fa-vor for the North. But in the interests of peace, he hoped that they would set aside the bitterness still lingering over the recent conflict with England and France in the Crimea and realize that the North's welfare (and that of everyone else) lay in calling off the war.[14]

In view of Lee's penetration of the North, Palmerston deemed it ad-visable to postpone action until the South had time to inflict a mortal wound inside the Union that would assure its consent to mediation. "It is evident," he wrote to Russell, "that a great conflict is taking place to the north-west of Washington, and its issue must have a great effect on the state of affairs. If the Federals sustain a great defeat they may be at once ready for mediation, and the Iron should be struck while it is hot. If, on the other hand, they should have the best of it, we may wait awhile and see what may follow."[15]

On the eve of what was shaping up as a major military encounter in Maryland, the British government had advanced toward a mediation that rested on the assumption of another Union defeat and that, for the first time, contained actual terms of settlement. On 24 September, Palmerston notified Gladstone of Russell's support for a mediation proposal that the ministry, with cabinet approval, should invite France and Russia to join. The terms were to be an armistice followed by the Union's lifting the blockade and entering negotiations based on southern separation. Gladstone learned two days later from Russell that he advocated an "offer of media-tion to both parties in the first place, and in the case of refusal by the North, to recognition of the South." A safeguard seemed necessary. Russell would support mediation "on the basis of separation and recognition ac-companied by a [renewed] declaration of neutrality." A cabinet meeting as early as 16 October would be suitable if he could communicate his and Palmerston's views to France and Russia in the interim. To his ambassador in Paris that same day, Russell wrote that England and France should invite Russia to participate. If the Union rejected a mediation offer, En-gland should extend recognition to the South while reaffirming neu-trality. "Palmerston agrees entirely in this course."[16]

Despite Russell's precautionary measures, the ministry's mediation proposal would unavoidably heighten the danger of war with the Union. His deliberations rested on three questionable assumptions: that Lee would win in the North, that the Union would capitulate, and that the White House would trust the British claim to disinterest. And, of course, mediation might begin as a sincere search for peace, but the monumental nature of an intervention had the potential of carrying the involvement beyond England's reassurances of continued neutrality. Doubtless Russell counted heavily—too heavily—on the North's inability to rebound from Second Bull Run and certain other expected losses stemming from Lee's assaults. Clearly Russell did not realize that any form of British involvement in American affairs spoke louder than a hundred verbal pledges of neutrality. Certainly he did not appreciate the significance of the Union's ongoing military successes in the West. And finally, the foreign secretary relied too heavily on Stuart's ill-informed assurances from Washington that the South would never relent and that the peace parties in the North would win the November congressional elections. But Russell felt confident that the weight of world opinion—even without Russian participation— would rest on the side of the peacemakers. Would not England, and others who joined in the mediation, ease suspicions of self-interest by reaffirming neutrality while extending recognition? And even if the Lincoln administration considered waging a war against the outsiders, the imminence of winter would force Washington's policymakers to give the matter more thought than if mediation came during the warm months. A reasonable man, Russell assumed that the leaders in the White House were equally reasonable. They would accept a separation.

Gladstone was pleased that the time had come for the European powers to end the American war. If the Confederates made additional military gains, he feared, they could themselves pose problems in the negotiations. England should first make "a friendly effort" to convince the North to quit the war before Lee's advancing forces aroused a strong southern sentiment and complicated the task of securing peace. If Europe failed to act, the South would conquer too much territory and want to hold on to its new possessions. Gladstone had another reason for immediate intervention. Textile workers in his native Lancashire had been suffering "with a fortitude and patience exceeding all example, and almost all belief." If their forbearance should break and violence erupt, the government would appear interested only in securing cotton and lose its claim to being an "influence for good." The United States would regard British intervention as an effort to expand their American holdings. Russian involvement would give the move "moral authority."[17]

While the Palmerston ministry prepared for mediation, Confederate and Union forces confronted each other on 17 September at Antietam, a creek lying outside the small village of Sharpsburg in Maryland that became the scene of the bloodiest single day's fighting in the Civil War. The South's first major effort to take the war into the North came to a sudden and brutal end in the course of a few hours as tens of thousands of soldiers engaged in deadly combat. By early evening, more than 24,000 Union and Confederate soldiers had been wounded or killed. Lee's army had sustained such heavy casualties that it limped back into Virginia on the evening of the following day, leaving Union general George B. McClellan's battered legions in possession of the battlefield.[18]

News of Antietam reached London in late September, at first disappointing the ministry by demonstrating again the North's determination to win and yet, paradoxically, lending support to a mediation intended to stop this growing bloodbath. Given the heightened British interest in some course of action, it seems more than coincidental that the Earl of Shaftesbury, who was the son-in-law of Lady Palmerston and widely known to be under the prime minister's influence, should pass through Paris about 23 September (*before* news of Antietam had reached Europe) to offer assurances, according to Confederate minister John Slidell, that British recognition was no more than a few weeks away. The South's drive for independence, Shaftesbury explained, had won the support of Englishmen who opposed the North's imperial interests. Indeed, on September 30 (*after* Antietam's news reached Europe), Shaftesbury assured Slidell that the British attitude had not changed: "There is every reason to believe that the event so strongly desired of which we talked when I had the pleasure of seeing you in Paris is very close at hand."[19]

If Adams was correct—that Shaftesbury was a "good key" to understanding British policy—the Battle of Antietam had *not* put the quietus on intervention. British observers were shocked by the South's poor showing, for they had hoped for another military success that would have compelled the North to accept mediation. Instead, the Union claimed victory and hardened its resolution. Although Antietam proved indecisive from a tactical point of view, it restored the Union's morale, so severely shaken at Second Bull Run. Indeed, news of the battle in Maryland had heightened the British call for an intervention that some said was needed now more badly than before.[20]

Antietam appeared to confirm the contemporary view that the American antagonists had become locked in a death grip that could be broken only by outside assistance. In Washington, Stuart interpreted the results at Antietam as a lethal stalemate. After the battle, he wrote Russell, McClellan had wanted to rest his army and, like the South, did not want the Potomac River behind him during this season of rain and swollen waters. The general had failed to achieve a victory because he refused to pursue the enemy. Antietam was therefore "as near a drawn Battle as could be, only that the Federals have since held the ground." Stuart persisted in his optimism. The war appeared to be moving toward a political revolution in the North that would carry the peace advocates to the front. Palmerston likewise thought the war had deadlocked, which was, he told Russell with some relief, "just the case for the stepping in of friends."[21]

England also came under French pressure to move toward a mediation. Within a week of the battle, Stuart prepared a dispatch containing French minister Henri Mercier's proposal that he and Lyons jointly declare their desire for an armistice that would enable North and South to discuss peace terms. The two ministers would be ready with their good offices if wanted, but England and France should consider themselves free to act according to their own interests. For strategic reasons, Mercier recommended avoiding the word "separation." He felt confident that an armistice would be accepted because, after the grisly outcome at Antietam, neither North nor South would want to resume hostilities. Stuart thought that Mercier's approach could be pursued with "perfect safety." It would have a favorable impact on the United States because, Stuart believed, most Americans now wanted peace.[22]

Thus was the Union victory at Antietam replete with ironies. At least in part to win a foreign involvement in the war, Lee had sought a victory in the North that failed on the battlefield but had, by reverse logic, intensified British interest in mediation. In the aftermath of the Union's narrow victory, Adams in London joined Seward in happily—and mistakenly—thinking that British interest in intervention had declined.[23] Lincoln also misread the situation. He became so convinced that Antietam had dealt a crippling blow to foreign intervention that he now prepared to play his trump card—a proclamation of emancipation that would sound the death knell to outside involvement. But unbeknownst to both the American embassy in London and the highest governing circles in Washington, Lee's defeat at Antietam and rumors of Lincoln's decision for emancipation had already combined with the growing horrors of the war to strengthen British interest in mediation.

Shortly after the Battle of Antietam came the president's preliminary proclamation of emancipation. On 22 September, timed as Seward had advised—in the immediate aftermath of a Union military victory—Lincoln announced that, as of 1 January 1863, all slaves in states still in rebellion were free. "No other step," he had recently told an antislavery delegation in Washington, "would be so potent to prevent foreign intervention." Lincoln thus recognized the acute inseparability of foreign and domestic affairs, as well as the integral relationship between diplomatic and military considerations. The proclamation was "a practical war measure," he explained in the *Chicago Tribune,* "to be decided upon according to the advantages or disadvantages it may offer to the suppression of the rebellion." Emancipation would convince Europe that "we are incited by something more than ambition."[24]

British suspicions of the Union's ulterior motives in emancipation were not entirely off the mark: Lincoln intended that this wartime measure undermine slavery and thus tear down the South from within. But no evidence suggests that he envisioned a Nat Turner–style revolt. He spoke only of black service in the Union army, mass flight from the plantations, and, to those slaves who remained, encouragement to cease work. To alleviate concern over the unrest that the measure would foment among the slaves, Lincoln made two additions to the proclamation at Seward's request—that freedmen be urged "to abstain from all violence, unless in necessary self-defense," and that, "in all cases, when allowed, they labor faithfully for reasonable wages." Further, in the hundred days between the preliminary and final proclamations, Lincoln had agreed to delete passages misinterpreted by many as a call for insurrection—those declaring that the executive would not restrict blacks in their attempt to secure freedom and those referring to colonization and compensated emancipation. The proclamation, however, was certain to raise the slaves' cry for freedom while intensifying southern resistance to the Union and thereby necessitating a war of subjugation. The British were partly correct. Lincoln did not want a full-scale racial upheaval, but he assured an official in the Department of Interior that "the [old] South is to be destroyed."[25]

Stuart reacted to the proclamation with disgust and raised again the apparition of slave revolts. The British chargé immediately wrote Russell that the decree applied only to areas still in rebellion and where the Union had no "*de facto* jurisdiction." One of Lincoln's chief motives in the proclamation, Stuart believed, was to "render intervention impossible." The move demonstrated no "pretext of humanity" and was "cold, vindictive, and entirely political." It offered "direct encouragement to servile insurrections."[26]

News of the president's proclamation reached England in early October, causing British spokesmen on all sides of the American issue to envision additional atrocities in the war. Emancipation, Russell learned from Stuart, had infuriated the Confederate Congress in Richmond and caused "threats of raising the Black Flag and other measures of retaliation." A northern governor had called for the importation of the French guillotine, and if Lincoln and the Republicans stayed in power, Stuart warned, "we may see reenacted some of the worst excesses of the French Revolution." From the Foreign Office in London, Permanent Under-Secretary Edmund Hammond (who was pro-South) likewise treated the proclamation with disdain. Even Member of Parliament Richard Cobden, who staunchly opposed slavery, had reservations about using emancipation as a military weapon. In attempting to prevent separation and the establishment of a slave nation, the North would "half ruin itself in the process of wholly ruining the South." To seek victory with black cooperation would lead to "one of the most bloody & horrible episodes in history." The English view attracted support from across the Channel. That same month, the French informed the Palmerston ministry that the threat of a slave uprising provided another reason for their willingness to work with England in ending the American war.[27]

ABE LINCOLN'S LAST CARD; OR, ROUGE-ET-NOIR.

(Punch, 18 Oct. 1862)

The British press reacted to the proclamation with uniform hostility. The *Times* of London sarcastically remarked: "Where he has no power Mr. Lincoln will set the negroes free; where he retains power he will consider them as slaves." The announcement was "more like a Chinaman beating his two swords together to frighten his enemy than like an earnest man pressing forward his cause." The London *Spectator* sympathized with the Union but was befuddled by its declaration regarding slavery: "The principle is not that a human being cannot justly own another, but that he cannot own him unless he is loyal to the United States." The *Bee-Hive* of London, which remained pro-South until a change in editors in January 1863, criticized the proclamation for attempting to free slaves in the South, where Lincoln had no authority, and leaving those in bondage where he did. In an editorial, the *Times* asked whether "the reign of the last PRESIDENT [was] to go out amid horrible massacres of white women and children, to be followed by the extermination of the black race in the South? Is LINCOLN yet a name not known to us as it will be known to posterity, and is it ultimately to be classed among that catalogue of monsters, the wholesale assassins and butchers of their kind?" *Blackwood's Magazine* of Edinburgh called the proclamation "monstrous, reckless, devilish." To win the war, "the North would league itself with Beelzebub, and seek to make a hell of half a continent."[28]

Palmerston, of course, was the central figure in a mediation decision, and if he had moved cautiously closer to taking such an action before Antietam, he now just as cautiously moved farther away. He remained confident that the South would accept mediation "upon the Basis of Separation," but, he assured Russell, the North would reject the offer because Antietam had deluded the Lincoln administration into believing that its war aims were attainable. The South had still not achieved a major battlefield success capable of compelling the North to accept mediation without demanding a war of revenge against England. The mediation offer "has been lately checked" by the Battle of Antietam, and England might have to wait another ten days for "future prospects." If the Union insisted on war with the mediating nation (or nations), it might be advisable to delay the offer until spring weather opened British communications to

Canada and permitted the Royal Navy to operate along the Atlantic coast. Perhaps the only way to avert an Anglo-American conflict resulting from a mediation would be to avoid a unilateral recognition of the South. "If the acknowledgement were made at one and the same time by England, France and some other Powers, the Yankee would probably not seek a quarrel with us alone, and would not like one against a European Confederation."[29]

To circumvent the dangers of a mediation, Palmerston devised a seemingly less provocative plan intended to highlight the atrocities at Antietam as a reason for peace while delaying any formal interventionist move until the South achieved a decisive victory on the battlefield. Before making an actual proposal of mediation, he wrote Russell, the British government should offer a "friendly suggestion" that the time was right for the two adversaries to consider whether a continuation of the war was wiser than to accept a separation "which must apparently be the inevitable result of the contest, however long it may last." Admittedly, armistice terms would be difficult to arrange. A cease-fire accompanied by the end of the blockade would help the South; one that retained the blockade would favor the North. But no matter how rancorous the armistice discussions might become, the North and South themselves must resolve the details. Any quarrels that developed during the negotiations, Palmerston declared, "would do us no harm if they did not lead to a renewal of war." At present, however, *in*action continued to be the best policy because neither side seemed ready for a cease-fire. "The whole matter is full of difficulty, and can only be cleared up by some more decided events between the contending armies."[30]

Russell, however, had become dissatisfied with Palmerston's hesitation and wanted to forge ahead without waiting for a Confederate military victory. The moment for action had come, he wrote the prime minister: "I think unless some miracle takes place this will be the very time for offering mediation, or as you suggest, proposing North and South to come to terms." A British proposal must make two points: that England recommended separation, and that it "shall take no part in the war unless attacked." Russell did not share Palmerston's concern that British acknowledgment of southern separation meant war with the Union. "My only doubt," he declared, "[was] whether we and France should stir if Russia holds back. Her separation from our move would ensure the rejection of our proposals." Yet he appeared willing to go ahead with France and without the Russians. Perhaps because of their likely absence, he suddenly became amenable to avoiding any mention of separation. He referred to Stuart's letter of 23 September, which expressed his and Mercier's call for an armistice proposal containing no reference to a separation. "If no fresh battles occur," Russell declared, "I think the suggestion might be adopted. . . . It would be a fair and defensible course, leaving it open to us to hasten or defer recognition if the proposal is declined."[31]

Thus the Battle of Antietam joined with the preliminary proclamation of emancipation to encourage Russell and others to seek intervention. In addition to humanitarian concerns, Russell feared that the endless nature of the fighting, compounded by a certain race war, might spread beyond the United States to involve other nations. Further, the war's continuance would soon cause an economic crisis in England stemming from a steadily decreasing cotton supply. Of more immediate importance, however, was his concern that the war would become racial as well as sectional. For months resentment had been growing in England over a suspected White House maneuver to steer the war into an antislavery channel for reasons having little or nothing to do with moral purpose. Since the president had waited so long to take a stand against slavery, Russell and many British observers believed that this decision now grew out of a desperate attempt to avert defeat by stirring up a slave rebellion. Lincoln and the Republican party, it appeared to many Englishmen, were prepared to capitalize on human bondage in order to destroy the South.

Seward had been correct: the British did regard emancipation as the dying gasp of the Union because the proclamation failed to follow a decisive Union victory in the field. The Union's margin of victory at Antietam was so thin that the British dismissed the proclamation as an act of desperation. Lincoln had "played his last card," according to the *Times*. "He will appeal to the black blood of the African; he will whisper of the pleasures of spoil and of the gratification of yet fiercer instincts; and when the blood begins to flow and shrieks come piercing through the darkness, Mr.

Lincoln will wait till the rising flames tell that all is consummated, and then he will rub his hands and think that revenge is sweet."[32]

Despite the long-standing belief that the Union victory at Antietam, followed by the preliminary proclamation of emancipation, had halted a move toward British intervention, the truth is that the coming of the battle only put on hold a mediation procedure well under way and then, when the results of the battle became known, encouraged Russell to depart from Palmerston's cautionary strictures to resume the move toward intervention. Union forces had turned back Lee's first major thrust into the North and earned them the right to claim a strategic victory. The administration in Washington had tried to take advantage of that outcome by announcing emancipation in an effort to preempt British intervention. But the battle and proclamation did not shake the interest of Russell, Gladstone, and numerous others outside the ministry in mediation. Antietam and the proclamation combined to raise the specter of a war of subjugation made even more horrible by a certain slave uprising.[33]

For Russell, the proclamation intensified his need to act. He now advocated a mediation based on an armistice that he knew would, as a matter of course, culminate in recognition. Russell had emerged as the chief advocate for stopping the war in the name of peace.

In preparation for an October cabinet meeting to discuss the interventionist issue, Russell wrote a memorandum to his colleagues urging support for an armistice. Gladstone had just delivered a fiery speech a few days before in Newcastle, leaving the erroneous impression that the ministry was on the verge of extending recognition to the South. In reality, he had spoken rashly and without authorization, but his action had inadvertently brought attention to the three greatest obstacles to such a move: how to step between the antagonists without becoming involved in the war, how to present a workable solution to the problem, and how to secure Russian participation. Russell, however, failed to grasp these complexities. Emancipation, he now argued in his memo, had authorized the Union armies to commit "acts of plunder, of incendiarism, and of revenge" that would destroy the South. The war must stop, but he knew that a British decision to bring this about depended on support from across the English Channel. Europe's great powers (England, France, Russia, Austria, and Prussia) had to decide whether intervention was justified in light of present conditions in America—the balance between military forces, indecisive but costly battles, heightened political hatreds, and a society enraged by Lincoln's effort to excite "the passions of the slave to aid the destructive progress of armies." Europe's duty, he declared, was to ask both the antagonists to lay down their arms and weigh the advantages of peace against continued bloodshed.[34]

Russell's most formidable opponent finally emerged in the person of Secretary for War Lewis, who had long been convinced that any form of British intervention would be a mistake. A gentle and unpretentious man, he was a philosopher-scholar of unquestionable integrity who commanded widespread respect because of his wisdom and devotion to justice and country. The American war had disturbed him from its beginning. He had never believed that military force could keep the Union intact. In January 1861, he had declared to a friend: "You may conquer an insurgent province, but you cannot conquer a seceding State." Secession, he confided to another friend, would lead to "arbitration of the sword." But Lewis staunchly opposed intervention—particularly before the Confederacy had proved its claim to nationhood. In a speech in Hereford followed by a memo sent to fellow cabinet members, Lewis insisted that the South had not yet established independence and warned that Russell's armistice proposal would not go to a "conclave of philosophers" but to the great mass of "heated and violent partizans" on both sides who bitterly opposed compromise. He agreed with Russell that Lincoln intended for emancipation to provoke a slave uprising in the South; but Lewis insisted that intervention meant war with the Union. Further, England as mediator had no peace terms to suggest. If any plan sanctioned slavery, the ministry would become its guarantor while alienating the North. If England called for abolition, the South would resist. Where would the boundary lie between North and South? How would England deal with the border states? With the territories? "The sword has not yet traced the conditions of a treaty recognizing the independence of the South."[35]

Lewis's argument only temporarily delayed Russell's call for an armistice, for French emperor Napoleon III soon made a proposal of his own. Russell had postponed the cabinet meeting after his peace plan drew little support from his colleagues, and he found France preoccupied with European problems. But he remained firmly convinced that it was the moral responsibility of the combined powers of England, France, Russia, and perhaps even Austria and Prussia to stop the American war. Then, in late October, Napoleon revived Russell's flickering hopes by proposing an Anglo-French-Russian mediation offer that included a six-month armistice and a suspension of the Union blockade. But the emperor had more—much more—in mind. Privately to Slidell, Napoleon added a dangerous twist to the proposal that, based on Russell's recent abortive involvement with France in Mexico, would not have been surprising if known: Union rejection of the joint offer, the emperor declared, would provide "good reason for recognition" and, in words carrying an obvious reference to the use of force, "perhaps for more active intervention."[36]

Lewis again led the opposition, this time with a second memo to the cabinet of 15,000 words and with a series of letters to the editor of the *Times* that his stepson-in-law, William Vernon Harcourt (later the first person to hold the Whewell Chair of International Law at Cambridge University), signed under the pseudonym of "Historicus." Lewis insisted (as did Harcourt) that intervention would cause war with the Union by allying England with the Confederacy in its drive for independence. Yet to achieve peace, Lewis admitted, international law permitted neutral nations to engage in "an avowed armed interference in a war already existing." But, he asked, would this approach be expedient and wise? The North remained powerful despite secession, and the European powers would have great difficulty in sending fleets and armies to the Potomac. How would they transport large armies across the Atlantic? How would Europe's wooden vessels fare against the North's ironclads? And even if Europe's great powers succeeded in forcing the North to recognize the South, new problems would arise at the peace table. The intervening nations would have to establish in Washington a "Conference of Plenipotentiaries of the Five Great Powers." What would be its makeup? If comprised of their five ministers then in Washington, it would not have enough weight. If Europe sent over new plenipotentiaries, they would lack intimate knowledge of American politics. Distance would also pose a problem. Would the plenipotentiaries act on their own, or would they have to refer back to their home governments for instructions on every issue? It was dangerous to grant unlimited powers of negotiation, but if not done, long delays would ensue that could only make matters worse.[37]

If the European powers used force to end the war, the ensuing Washington Conference (as Lewis called it) would have to formulate peace terms, a problem already raised in his October memo. "These and other thorny questions would have to be settled by a Conference of five foreigners, acting under the daily fire of the American press." And even if the five powers intervened in concert, how long would that concert last? Such a conference would be "an imposing force," Lewis admitted, "but it [was] a dangerous body to set in motion." The powers would not only have to satisfy the North and South but themselves as well. As in Belgium's recent trouble, Austria, Prussia, and Russia might take one side, and England and France the other. "England might stand alone."[38]

Lewis's long memo killed the French proposal and prompted a decisive British turn away from intervention in the American war. On 11–12 November, the cabinet met and, after a bitter debate punctuated by Russell's revelation that Russia refused to participate, overwhelmingly rejected Napoleon's offer. Then, as time approached for implementing the Emancipation Proclamation, a curious change in British attitude became evident: public indignation over Lincoln's move unexpectedly eased with the slow realization that slavery's end was in sight. To the north of London, workers gathered in huge rallies beginning in December 1862, cheering the North and proclaiming the rights of workers everywhere. For weeks, Adams was besieged with petitions, resolutions, and letters from working groups (and emancipation societies), all supporting the president's action.[39]

More than a few British spokesmen remained infuriated with what they continued to regard as the Union's hypocrisy concerning slavery and only grudgingly joined the swelling flood of support for the North. The Emancipation Proclamation made that task easier. In only that sense did Lincoln's move against slavery have an important impact on England.

The British decision to stay out of the war proved crucial to the collapse of the Confederacy. Before 1863, when talk of intervention was at its height, the verdict of the war hung in the balance. Had the British chosen to intervene, the South would have won recognition, and dissident groups in the North would have been strengthened in their opposition to the war. The Confederacy would have secured enough outside military and commercial aid to have prolonged its resistance—and perhaps to have won independence. One cannot conclude with certainty that recognition would have changed the war's ultimate judgment. And yet, recognition would have provided a morale boost to the South at a pivotal time in the war, heightened its chances for floating loans abroad and raising more money at home, assured foreign challenges to the Union blockade as neutral vessels attempted to trade with the South, and, as a matter of course, brought about a third war between the Atlantic nations that would have facilitated permanent disunion and severely damaged Anglo-American relations for years to come.

No one can dispute the argument that a British intervention in the Civil War would have profoundly affected its outcome. But can we automatically assume that such an involvement would have guaranteed the longevity of the romanticized Old South as immortalized in Margaret Mitchell's epic novel *Gone with the Wind?* Though many southerners continue to mourn what might have been, the probability is that the Confederacy of their dreams would have vanished as quickly as it did in the real world of 1865. An examination of the facts demonstrates that the British never considered intervention *on behalf of the South*. In no way could they have condoned the prolonged existence of slavery. Even had they compromised by approving a gradual emancipation program, the result would have been the establishment of the only slave nation north of the equator, and one rimmed by a free republic (itself reduced in territorial size and population by more than a third) while tied to agriculture in a world becoming increasingly industrialized and more liberal in social and political concerns. The conclusion is inescapable: British intervention in the war would have damaged *both* North and South while benefiting the interests of England in the hemisphere as well of those of France and any other Continental powers joining the venture.

Fortunately, in 1862 history took precedence over mythology. The British refused to intervene, and once they did, the French followed suit, meaning that this most horrible of wars, as the Palmerston ministry termed the American conflict, had to grind on to its end at Appomattox Courthouse in April 1865.[40]

QUESTION: As an amateur historian, I have always felt that one question is the key to historical analysis: Is humanity basically good or basically evil? If you answer the latter affirmatively, then, from that perspective, what was the advantage in intervention for Britain? Certainly the British were not going to mediate the Civil War for purely altruistic motives. I can understand France wanting to make Maximilian a success in Mexico. But what was the British motive?

ANSWER: Russell looked at the matter in a very complex way. First, he and Palmerston and Lewis and all the others did not fully understand the war. What could drive brother to kill brother? Here were the British exalting themselves as the most civilized nation in the world, three thousand miles away in the Victorian Age, looking at these events in America and saying that it was the responsibility of a civilized country to do something about what they called the most horrible of wars. Russell was moved by a mixture of motives. Certainly he was concerned about the economic ramifications of a war that seemed endless. He also knew that southern cotton and northern wheat were vital links in a chain of world economic development. If the South were to be subjugated, and the Cotton Kingdom destroyed, the impact would be devastating.

Unfortunately for the Confederacy, the South had two bumper crops before the war and had sold tremendous amounts of cotton to the British. So the war was, in a very crude sense, a godsend to some English business-men. Now they could dump their surplus cotton, lay off their workers, and charge higher prices. But this supply was going to run out in about eighteen months, in late 1862 or early 1863. The British were already looking for other sources for cotton, but they preferred the South's high-quality cotton, and the North knew this. The North therefore confiscated cotton and sent it to England in an effort to reduce any cotton stress.

Russell was also concerned about the bloodshed of the war—but *not* to the point of entering the war because he felt sorry for the Americans. He believed that for a mixture of humanitarian, economic, and strategic rea-sons, England as a civilized nation had a responsibility to do something to stop the war.

QUESTION: Is it not difficult to determine which groups of British citi-zens favored whom in the war?

ANSWER: This is a very good point: it is really difficult to define British opinion. There was every range of opinion about this war. But what I have found especially interesting is that a large group of British observers—including Palmerston—felt that this monstrous war spawned at Fort Sumter had to come to an end. The best way to end this war, most seemed to believe, was to recognize that the North could not possibly subjugate the South. Its territory and population were too large. Let it go, and let it become a slave republic! Russell argued that this very simple solution would avoid further bloodshed. The South would then be com-pletely surrounded by free territory and sooner or later would have to join the nineteenth century by giving up slavery. And wouldn't it be better to do it this way?

This observation by Russell provides an excellent illustration of his inability to understand the war. The North and the South had irreconcilable differences, the former insisting on Union and the latter demanding independence. The only solution, both sides believed, was the "final solution"—war.

QUESTION: I was wondering if Russell was concerned that if there were a slave revolt, this might spark revolts throughout the British Empire, particularly in India?

ANSWER: I think you have a good point. Russell probably was concerned about the example that a slave revolution in the South would set for the British Empire. What would happen in India? What would happen in Ireland? What would happen in a number of places throughout the world? There is a great deal of evidence that Russell, when he spoke in the House of Lords in early 1862 about his concerns, did worry about the mutiny by the Sepoys of India just five years earlier. This apprehension weighed heavily on the minds of British legislators as well.

The British were concerned about the implications of the events in America from the first day of the war. They first assumed that the war was about slavery. Then Lincoln, for political reasons, denied that the war concerned slavery. And the South, of course, sent representatives to England, who insisted that the war was about southern independence and northern aggression, not slavery. And then the *Times* of London joined others in comparing the war in America to the war of the 1770s and 1780s between England and the colonies. They agreed that this was a war of northern aggression against a move for southern independence—much like the one in the colonies, which was, they had to admit, a war of oppression by the king and Parliament. So they began talking about letting the South go. What would be wrong with that? There were, after all, separate countries in Europe. But then, of course, Lincoln changed the war into one of slavery and antislavery, convincing the British that the dire predictions they had been hearing were true: Lincoln intended to destroy the South from within by stirring up slave revolts.

QUESTION: How much did the opening up of new markets—Egypt and other places—for cotton dissuade the interventionist move?

ANSWER: I think it did a great deal. In fact, some leading members of Parliament thought it good to be denied access to southern cotton because it would force them to break their dependence upon a single source and find others. Who knew how long that single source would last? That had to take some of the steam out of the interventionist movement.

QUESTION: Were there people in England who did not support emancipation because they worried that the emancipation of the slaves in the South would ruin the cotton economy forever?

ANSWER: Yes, there were people worried about the end of the Cotton Kingdom and the flow of cotton to England. But we by no means have a thorough collection of documents that reveals all aspects of the British reaction to the war. It was simply regarded as the most horrible thing that one had ever seen. Russell had read about the Battle of Shiloh of early April 1862, and then this atrocity had been followed by Antietam. The specter of these events was unbelievable. Indeed, English observers came to America to watch these armies. And Palmerston was horrified when the Union built the ironclads, and immediately wanted the British navy to acquire them. There were certainly many British observers, I would guess, who did not support slavery but who felt that if it came to an end, they would lose a valuable source of cotton. Who would take the place of slaves in working the economy?

QUESTION: What did the South do with propaganda to try to encourage intervention?

ANSWER: The first thing the South did was send William Yancey from Alabama, who was one of the most outspoken proponents of slavery and secession, on a diplomatic mission to London, accompanied by two who were cut out of just about the same mold. They went to England, where Yancey astounded the British by being calm and mannered. And he argued that the war was not about slavery but about southern independence.

The South also sent Henry Hotze to England with the authorization to establish a propaganda newspaper in London called the *Index*.

QUESTION: How would you compare southern and northern diplomacy?

ANSWER: The South based its diplomacy on "King Cotton." Southerners warned the British that if they did not support the Confederacy, the cotton flow would stop. The South, however, ran up against the fact that the British had a year and a half or two years of surplus supplies. So that threat did not carry much weight. Then the South sent James Mason over as the first official emissary of the Confederacy. Mason arrived in England and immediately undermined the British image of the South as populated by Robert E. Lees—dignified men with nicely combed hair and beautiful white beards, chivalrous gentlemen out of Sir Walter Scott novels. Mason was disheveled, and he was rude and obnoxious, fully expecting to sit in the front seat of the chamber—where visitors to Parliament were not allowed to sit—because he represented the Confederate States of America. To top it off, he chewed tobacco, which was as distasteful as anything the British could imagine; moreover, he spat the tobacco in Parliament and more often than not missed the spittoon and landed it in a heap on the red carpet. And this was the chief diplomat of the South.

However, in all fairness to Mason, the South could have sent the best diplomat imaginable, and he still could have done little more for the South. Again, I repeat, I do not think the British ever saw enough in it to intervene. I do not think that anyone could have persuaded the British to act against their own interests. Certainly Mason could not have done anything. Still, the South's diplomacy was not the best.

The Union, on the other hand, had Lincoln as the chief diplomat. The Union had William Seward, and Seward was outspoken. He could cuss out a person without a moment's hesitation. He told the British that if they intervened, there would be war. And he made sure this warning got to England. Lyons thought Seward was a loose cannon, capable of anything. At receptions, Seward drank whiskey and smoked cigars so incessantly that one could barely see him through the smoke; but it was clear where he was because of the noise. And Seward did this on purpose. There's no question about it.

I see a similarity between Seward and Lincoln in the 1860s and Dulles and Eisenhower in the 1950s. Seward functioned as a lightning rod, and Lincoln was a great peacemaker; and in this century, Dulles was a lightning rod, and Eisenhower kept things under control. Lincoln knew what Seward was doing, but he let him do it because it was excellent diplomacy to convince the British that intervention meant war. They could not even talk about a mediation—which was simply sitting down to talk—because to mediate meant bestowing equality onto the South. That would have been tantamount to recognition, to saying that secession worked and the Constitution was dead. Lincoln believed fervently in the Union. He was a strong advocate of Daniel Webster and Henry Clay. Lincoln had a religious view about the Union: like martyrs who die for their faith, the more the North lost in the war, the stronger its Union sentiment became. The British could never fathom Lincoln's devotion to the Union.

QUESTION: Did Canadian opinion have much influence on British feeling during the war?

ANSWER: Seward made sure the British knew that Canada would be the first area of retaliation if they interfered. If there was war, he promised, Union soldiers would be on their way to Canada. In the War of 1812, Americans had invaded Canada, and even though they never accomplished its conquest, there was always this threat that the Americans could move north by way of the Great Lakes and the St. Lawrence. In the 1860s the British realized that if they wanted to operate against the Union in Atlantic waters, they would have to do so out of Canadian territory.

QUESTION: You mentioned the logistics of moving troops across the Atlantic. What was the status of the British military at the time? Given the blockade, could the British have moved their troops to America?

ANSWER: My answer has to be speculative. I would guess that there was no way that the British army could match the numbers amassed by the Union. Not many countries could match the Union force in this war. And then there were the ironclads. The British did not have ironclads. The Union's ironclads were not seaworthy, by any means, but the image they conjured up just horrified Palmerston. He respected and feared them and did not want to challenge them. Moreover, the British knew that if they intervened, they would have to challenge the blockade. They did not relish moving troops across the ocean, setting up headquarters, and so on. Palmerston and Lewis did not want to face such a horrendous task. Lewis was the one man who would have to do it, and he did not want to challenge the Union.

QUESTION: After the Emancipation Proclamation, did southerners encourage the British to believe that slave revolts were going to take place?

ANSWER: I did not find a great deal of evidence of this, but there were the statements by members of the Confederate Congress at Richmond that this was indeed going to happen. I think southerners considered this a given fact that they did not have to repeat. They did, however, offer to emancipate their slaves in exchange for British recognition. This offer came as late as March 1865, which points to how poor Confederate diplomacy was. Mason tried to strike this deal with Palmerston—

one that came from Jefferson Davis. Davis did not like the idea, but he went along with it out of desperation. The South intended to send a secret mission to London to make this arrangement. Even though the news of Appomattox had not yet reached Britain, Palmerston refused to negotiate, for he considered the war over after Gettysburg in July 1863. The South tried everything possible to get the British to extend recognition. Palmerston at one point asked Mason in exasperation what he hoped to gain from it. Mason said the South did not want men and supplies; it just wanted Britain to recognize the South. Palmerston could not understand this, and I cannot, either. I do not know what he was hoping to gain— certainly a morale boost and stature, but the South had to have men and everything else that goes with men to win the war.

QUESTION: If you had been Davis, whom would you have selected as minister to England?

ANSWER: I do not know who in the South would have been a good diplomat. I do not think that anyone could have matched the Union representative, Charles Francis Adams, and all the advantages he had. Adams was a premier diplomat. He was a cultured, well-read gentleman who knew how to move gracefully among British circles, which was not an easy thing to do. He was invited to parties, where he rubbed shoulders with the Palmerstons, and he talked to Russell all the time. I do not think that anyone could have outdone Adams.

I am convinced that treaties and good diplomatic relations result not so much from the person but from the conditions in which the person moves. Back in the 1790s, John Jay was a fine diplomat, but he could not secure the treaty with Britain that Americans wanted because the conditions were not right. He lacked leverage, or a strong bargaining position with the British. Thomas Pinckney was mediocre, but he negotiated a superb treaty with Spain because the conditions were right. The conditions were not right for the South. Recognition would have come at too high a price for the British.

QUESTION: Who was the chief architect of Confederate diplomacy?

ANSWER: Judah P. Benjamin, once he became secretary of state, was an outstanding person. He was very qualified, an exceptionally gifted man. But again, a diplomat must have some sort of leverage. This is the key in diplomacy. The South's leverage, it thought, was King Cotton. And King Cotton was simply no leverage.

QUESTION: Do we have a similar situation regarding Yugoslavia today? Can interventionism ever work?

ANSWER: People need to learn more about what Lewis wrote in his memo because it offers a universal way to look at this question. Essentially, he said that intervention often seems very simple. It seemed simple in the 1960s when Americans intervened in Vietnam. Drop a few bombs and send a few troops, many argued, and it will be all over. Russell and others had a simple answer during the Civil War: They would go to the United States and force the adversaries to sit down and talk. If they refused, the British would threaten physical force. And the Americans would sit down, and then what? What would the British tell them? What would the terms be? It is never very simple, and that is what Lewis was trying to point out. It is the same in any situation, in Bosnia, for example. It is never simple when one country intervenes in another country. I would hope that everyone considering intervention would set up worst-case scenarios, as Lewis did. Lewis persuaded Palmerston that there was no way to intervene effectively in the war. The result would most certainly be a war between England and the Union.

NOTES

1. James M. McPherson, *Battle Cry of Freedom: The Civil War Era* (New York, 1988), 545, 556–57; Stephen W. Sears, *Landscape Turned Red: The Battle of Antietam* (New York, 1983), 334; Frank L. Owsley, *King Cotton Diplomacy: Foreign Relations of the Confederate States of America* (Chicago, 1931; 2d ed., revised by Harriet C. Owsley, 1959), 347. See also D. P. Crook, *The North, the South, and the Powers, 1861–1865* (New York, 1974), 224–25.

2. For an expanded treatment of this argument, see my *Union in Peril: The Crisis over British Intervention in the Civil War* (Chapel Hill, 1993). See also Ephraim D. Adams, *Great Britain and the American Civil War,* 2 vols. (New York, 1925), 2:97–105; Brian Jenkins, *Britain & the War for the Union,* 2 vols. (Montreal, 1974–89), 2: 152–55. For the counterargument that the proclamation of emancipation had no major impact on British public opinion, see Joseph M. Hernon, Jr., "British Sympathies in the American Civil War: A Reconsideration," *Journal of Southern History* 33 (1967): 356–67. Kinley J. Brauer argues that Antietam exemplified the war's futility and thereby explains the British move toward mediation. See his "British Mediation and the American Civil War: A Reconsideration," *Journal of Southern History* 38 (1972): 50–51.

3. See Henry Blumenthal, "Confederate Diplomacy: Popular Notions and International Realities," *Journal of Southern History* 32 (1966): 151–71; Jefferson Davis, *The Rise and Fall of the Confederate Government,* 2 vols. (New York, 1881), 2:368–70. Not until the early twentieth century did nations distinguish between *de facto* and *de jure* recognition. See Hersh Lauterpacht, *Recognition in International Law* (Cambridge, England, 1947), 332. A *de facto* government is, in fact, in control, regardless of arguments about its legality. A *de jure* government is considered lawful, even though it may not be in actual control. Kenneth Bourne considers the period of British neutrality during the Civil War one of the most dangerous times in Anglo-American relations since the War of 1812. See his *Britain and the Balance of Power in North America, 1815–1908* (Berkeley, 1967), 210, 252–53. On the role of mediation as a possible outgrowth of making good offices available to promote the settlement of differences, see Henry Wheaton, *The Elements of International Law* (Philadelphia and London, 1836; 8th ed., Richard Henry Dana, Jr., ed., Boston, 1866), part 3, section 288.

4. Russell to Lyons, 21 March 1861, no. 69, William E. Gladstone Papers, British Library, Additional Manuscripts, 44, 593, vol. 508, London, England. See also A. Wyatt Tilby, *Lord John Russell: A Study in Civil and Religious Liberty* (London, 1930), 197; Russell to Lord Cowley (British ambassador to Paris), 15 April 1865, Russell Papers, PRO 30/22/106, Public Record Office, Kew, England; William H. Seward to C. F. Adams, 27 April 1861, no. 4, U.S. Department of State, *Papers Relating to Foreign Affairs: 1861* (Washington, D.C., 1861), 83 (hereafter cited as *FRUS*); Palmerston to Queen Victoria, 1 Jan. 1861, in Jasper Ridley, *Lord Palmerston* (New York, 1971), 548; Russell to Lyons, 10 Jan. 1861, Russell Papers, PRO 30/22/96. The *Bee Hive* of London also thought that the creation of two American republics would remedy the slavery question. See issues of 23 Nov., 7 Dec. 1861, cited in Philip S. Foner, *British Labor and the American Civil War* (New York, 1981), 29. British conservatives agreed with this analysis. See Donald Bellows, "A Study of British Conservative Reaction to the American Civil War," *Journal of Southern History* 51 (1985): 512–13, 522.

5. Parliamentary member John Bright, who favored the North, believed that violation of the blockade would mean war. See Bright to Richard Cobden, 16 Nov. 1861, 10 Jan. 1862, Bright Papers, Brit. Lib., Add. Mss., 43, 384, vol. 2. See also Bright to Cobden, 6, 9, 13 Jan. 1862, ibid.; Cobden to Bright, 8 Jan. 1862, Cobden Papers, Brit. Lib., Add. Mss., 43, 652, vol. 6; Jenkins, *Britain & War for Union,* 1: 243.

6. Lyons to Russell, 4 Oct. 1861, Russell Papers, PRO 30/22/35; Lyons to Russell, 23 May, 9 June 1862, ibid., PRO 30/22/36.

7. Russell to Lyons, 29 Dec. 1860, ibid., PRO 30/22/96; E. D. Adams, *GB and Civil War,* 1:217–72; Lyons to Russell, 20 Jan. 1862, quoted in ibid., 2:80. Russell's warning of a race war perhaps reminded his listeners of the rebellion in Haiti of the 1790s, the disappointing impact of emancipation on the West Indian colonies, the Sepoy rebellion in India of 1857, and England's ongoing problems in Ireland. For the sources of England's racial fears, see Crook, *North, South, and Powers,* 237–38; and McPherson, *Battle Cry of Freedom,* 558.

8. Seward to C. F. Adams, 28 May 1862, no. 260, U.S. Department of State, Despatches from U.S. Ministers to Great Britain, 1792–1870, National Archives, Washington, D.C. [hereafter cited as Disp., GB (NA)].

9. Stuart to Russell, 21, 29 July, 4 Aug. 1862, Russell Papers, PRO 30/22/36; Postmaster General Montgomery Blair to Lincoln, 23 July 1862, in Roy P. Basler, ed., *Collected Works of Abraham Lincoln,* 8 vols. and index (New Brunswick, 1953–55), 5:337 n. 1 [hereafter cited as *CWL*]; David Donald, ed., *Inside Lincoln's Cabinet: The Civil War Diaries of Salmon P. Chase* (New York, 1954), 99–100; Russell to Stuart, 25 July 1862, Russell Papers, PRO 30/22/96; Russell to Stuart, 7 Aug. 1862, Great Britain, *British Parliamentary Papers, 1801–1899: American Civil War,* 1,000 vols. (Shannon, Ireland, date varies by vol.), 17:29; Stuart to Seward, 30 Aug. 1862, with enclosure: Russell to Stuart, 28 July 1862, U.S. Department of State, Notes from the British Legation in the U.S. to the Department of State, 1791–1906 (National Archives). See also Kinley J. Brauer, "The Slavery Problem in the Diplomacy of the American Civil War," *Pacific Historical Review* 41 (1977): 450. Stuart was in charge of the British embassy in Washington, since Lyons had returned to London for a time due to poor health.

10. Seward to C. F. Adams, 28 July 1862, no. 308, *FRUS: 1862* (1863), 156–58.

11. Thouvenel cited in McPherson, *Battle Cry of Freedom,* 554. On Second Bull Run, see John J. Hennessy, *Return to Bull Run: The Campaign and Battle of Second Manassas* (New York, 1993).

12. *Times, Morning Post,* and *Morning Herald* all dated 16 September 1862 and cited in Jenkins, *Britain & War for Union,* 2:151; ibid., 167; Palmerston to Russell, 14 Sept. 1862, Russell Papers, PRO 30/22/14D; Russell to Palmerston, 17 Sept. 1862, GC/RU/728 (General Correspondence with Russell), Palmerston Papers, U. of Southampton, England.

13. Palmerston to Russell, 22 Sept. 1862, Russell Papers, PRO 30/22/14D; Russell to Palmerston, 22 Sept. 1862, GC/RU/729, Palmerston Papers.

14. Palmerston to Russell, 23 Sept. 1862, Russell Papers, PRO 30/22/14D. One author erroneously insists that by mid-September Palmerston was still not aware of Russia's opposition to intervention or of Seward's dependence on Russia for assistance. See Benjamin P. Thomas, *Russo-American Relations 1815–1867* (Baltimore, 1930), chap. 8.

15. Palmerston to Russell, 23 Sept. 1862, Russell Papers, PRO 30/22/14D.

16. Palmerston to Gladstone, 24 Sept. 1862, quoted in John Morley, *The Life of William Ewart Gladstone,* 3 vols. (London, 1903), 2:76; Russell to Gladstone, 26 Sept. 1862, Gladstone Papers, Brit. Lib., Add. Mss., 44, 292, vol. 207; Russell to Cowley, 26 Sept. 1862, Russell Papers, PRO 30/33/105.

17. Gladstone to Palmerston, 25 Sept. 1862, Gladstone Papers, Brit. Lib., Add. Mss., 44, 272, vol. 187.

18. McPherson, *Battle Cry of Freedom,* 545. See also James V. Murfin, *The Gleam of Bayonets: The Battle of Antietam and the Maryland Campaign of 1862* (New York, 1965); and Sears, *Landscape Turned Red.*

19. Charles Francis Adams, Jr., claims that news of Antietam reached England on 26 September. See his "The Crisis of Foreign Intervention in the War of Secession, September–November, 1862," *Massachusetts Historical Society Proceedings* 47 (1914): 32. Lynn M. Case and Warren F. Spencer show that the first stories of Antietam appeared in the Paris *Moniteur* on 27 and 30 September 1862. See their *The United States and France: Civil War Diplomacy* (Philadelphia, 1970), 339–40. In England, Minister Adams's assistant secretary, Benjamin Moran, first referred to the Union victory in his diary entry of 30 September; Moran Diary, 12 (30 Sept. 1862), Manuscript Division, Library of Congress, Washington, D.C. For the Shaftesbury episode, see Slidell to Judah P. Benjamin, 29 Sept. 1862, U.S. Naval War Records Office, *Official Records of the Union and Confederate Navies in the War of the Rebellion,* 2d ser., 3 vols. (Washington, D.C., 1894–1927), 3:546 [hereafter cited as *ORN*]; and Slidell to Benjamin, 9 Oct. 1862, ibid., 551.

20. For Adams's assessment of Shaftesbury, see Adams to Edward Everett, 2 May 1862, Adams Letterbook, Adams Family Papers, Massachusetts Historical Society, Boston, Mass.

21. Stuart to Russell, 29 Sept. 1862, Russell Papers, PRO 30/22/36; Palmerston to Russell, 30 Sept. 1862, ibid., PRO 30/33/14D.

22. Stuart to Russell, 23 Sept. 1862, ibid., PRO 30/22/36; Case and Spencer, *U.S. and France,* 326–28, 338.

23. C. F. Adams to Seward, no. 229, 3 Oct. 1862, *FRUS: 1862,* 205; Seward to C. F. Adams, no. 372, 18 Oct. 1862, ibid., 212–13.

24. Seward to C. F. Adams, no. 336, 8 Sept. 1862, ibid., 188; Seward to C. F. Adams, circular, 22 Sept. 1862, ibid., 195; Donald, ed., *Inside Lincoln's Cabinet,* 149–51 (22 Sept. 1862); "Preliminary Emancipation Proclamation," 22 Sept. 1862, *CWL,* 5:434; Lincoln, "Reply to Emancipation Memorial Presented by Chicago Christians of All Denominations, 13 Sept. 1862, ibid., 419–23; *Chicago Tribune,* 23 Sept. 1862, cited in ibid., 419 n.1; Jenkins, *Britain & War for Union,* 2:153; John Hope Franklin, *The Emancipation Proclamation* (Garden City, N.Y., 1963), 129–40; McPherson, *Battle Cry of Freedom,* 510, 557–58; Stephen B. Oates, "'The Man of Our Redemption':

Abraham Lincoln and the Emancipation of the Slaves," *Presidential Studies Quarterly* 9 (1979): 17, 19–20. On Lincoln's opposition toward slavery, see LaWanda Cox, *Lincoln and Black Freedom: A Study in Presidential Leadership* (Columbia, S.C., 1981); James M. McPherson, *Abraham Lincoln and the Second American Revolution* (New York, 1991); and Garry Wills, *Lincoln at Gettysburg: The Words That Remade America* (New York, 1992). Wills demonstrates Lincoln's attempt to implement the republican ideals of the Declaration of Independence.

25. Brauer, "Slavery Problem," 467; Glyndon G. Van Deusen, *William Henry Seward* (New York, 1967), 333; Roland C. McConnell, "From Preliminary to Final Emancipation Proclamation: The First Hundred Days," *Journal of Negro History* 48 (1963): 275; Tyler Dennett, ed., *Lincoln and the Civil War in the Diaries and Letters of John Hay* (New York, 1939), 50 (26 Sept. 1862); Lincoln quoted in T. J. Barnett to Samuel L. M. Barlow, 25 Sept. 1862, cited in McPherson, *Battle Cry of Freedom,* 558.

26. Stuart also told Lyons (then in London) of the Confederate retreat in Maryland and of the announcement of the preliminary proclamation of emancipation. Stuart to Lyons, 23 Sept. 1862, Russell Papers, PRO 30/22/36; Stuart to Russell, 23, 26 Sept. 1862, ibid. The Russian minister to the United States, Baron Edouard de Stoeckl, believed that Lincoln used the proclamation as a military tool against the South and not as a means for promoting freedom. See Stoeckl to Russian foreign minister, Prince Alexander Gorchakov, 25 Sept. 1862, cited in Brauer, "Slavery Problem," 463.

27. Stuart to Russell, 7 Oct. 1862, Russell Papers, PRO 30/22/36; Hammond to Sir Austen Henry Layard (under-secretary for foreign affairs), 6 Oct. 1862, Layard Papers, Brit. Lib., Add. Mss., 38, 951, vol. 21; Cobden to Bright, 6 Oct. 1862, Cobden Papers, Brit. Lib., Add. Mss., 43, 652, vol. 6; E. D. Adams, *GB and Civil War,* 2:103 n. 5. A few days later, Stuart wrote Russell that the proclamation of emancipation seemed to be causing many in the Union armies and the border states to desert to the South. Stuart to Russell, 10 Oct. 1862, Russell Papers, PRO 30/22/36.

28. Richard A. Heckman, "British Press Reaction to the Emancipation Proclamation," *Lincoln Herald* 71 (1969):150–53; *Times,* 7 Oct. 1862; *Spectator* [London, n.d.], quoted in Arnold Whitridge, "British Liberals and the American Civil War," *Civil War History* 22 (1976): 341; *Times,* 21 Oct. 1862; *Blackwood's Magazine* (Edinburgh), Oct.– Nov. 1862.

29. Palmerston to Russell, 2, 3 Oct. 1862, Russell Papers, PRO 30/22/14D.

30. Ibid., both references; Jenkins, *Britain & War for Union,* 2:170. Frank J. Merli shows Palmerston's reluctance to consider mediation after the Battle of Antietam. See Merli's *Great Britain and the Confederate Navy, 1861–1865* (Bloomington, 1970), 118, 257, 259.

31. Russell to Palmerston, 2, 4, 6 Oct. 1862, GC/RU/731–33, Palmerston Papers. The Russian ambassador in London, Baron Philip Brunow, was struck by the Palmerston ministry's insistence upon "doing something" before Parliament

reconvened after the first of the year. Gorchakov had already informed Stoeckl that Russia would not jeopardize its friendship with the United States. Brunow quote and Gorchakov citation in E. D. Adams, *GB and Civil War*, 2:45 n. 2.

32. *Times*, 6 Oct. 1862.

33. Seward to C. F. Adams, no. 359, 26 Sept. 1862, *FRUS: 1862*, 202.

34. Russell, "Memorandum" for Foreign Office, 13 Oct. 1862, in Gladstone Papers, Brit. Lib., Add. Mss., 44, 595, vol. 510; E. D. Adams, *GB and Civil War*, 2:49–50.

35. Gilbert F. Lewis, ed., *Letters of the Right Hon. Sir George Cornewall Lewis* (London, 1970), vi, viii–ix; Earl of Aberdeen to Lewis, 6 Nov. 1858, ibid., 352; Lewis to E. Twisleton (first friend), 21 Jan. 1861, ibid., 391–92; Lewis to Sir Edmund Head, governor of Canada (second friend), 10 March 1861, ibid., 393; Lewis to Head, 13 May 1861, ibid., 395; Lewis to Head, 8 Sept. 1861, ibid., 402; Head to Twisleton, 30 Nov. 1861, ibid., 405–6; characterization of Lewis by Duke of Argyll, in Duchess of Argyll, ed., *George Douglas, Eighth Duke of Argyll (1823–1900) Autobiography and Memoirs*, 2 vols. (London, 1906), 1:540; Lewis at Hereford in C. F. Adams, Jr., "Crisis of Foreign Intervention," 37; Lewis, "Memorandum on the American Question," 17 Oct. 1862, in Gladstone Papers, Brit. Lib., Add. Mss., 44, 595, vol. 510. Rumors were that Palmerston arranged for Lewis to deliver the speech at Hereford. Such rumors now seem unfounded. See E. D. Adams, *GB and Civil War*, 2:50, 50 n.1; Crook, *North, South, and Powers*, 233.

36. Russell to Stuart, 18 [?] Oct. 1862, Russell Papers, PRO 30/22/96; Russell to Cowley, 18 Oct. 1862, ibid., PRO 30/22/96; Russell to Cowley, 18 Oct. 1862, ibid., PRO 30/22/105; Russell to Palmerston, 18, 20, 24 Oct. 1862, GC/RU/734–36, Palmerston Papers; Palmerston to Russell, 20, 21, 22 Oct. 1862, Russell Papers, PRO 30/22/14D; Russell, "Memorandum"; Cowley to Russell, 27 Oct. 1862, Russell Papers, PRO 30/22/14D; Cowley's memorandum of his conversation with Edouard Drouyn de Lhuys, new French foreign minister, 28 Oct. 1862, GB, Foreign Office, France, General Correspondence, FO 27/1446, PRO; memo of Slidell interview with Napoleon on 28 Oct. 1862, enclosure B in Slidell to Benjamin, 28 Oct. 1862, *ORN*, 3:574–77; Case and Spencer, *U.S. and France*, 356–57; Owsley, *King Cotton Diplomacy*, 333–36; Russell to Palmerston, GC/RU/739, 3 Nov. 1862, Palmerston Papers. In late 1861, England had joined France and Spain in an expedition to Mexico that started as an effort to collect debts but soon took on a military cast that England and Spain quickly abandoned. France remained in Mexico until 1867.

37. Lewis, "Recognition of the Independence of the Southern States of the North American Union," 7 Nov. 1862, Gladstone Papers, Brit. Lib., Add. Mss., 44, 595, vol. 510 (original draft, though incomplete, in George Cornewall Lewis Papers, War Office and India, 3509, 3510, and 3514, National Library of Wales, Aberystwyth); A. G. Gardiner, *The Life of Sir William Harcourt*, 2 vols. (New York, 1923), 1:125, 127, 132–37; Jenkins, *Britain & War for Union*, 2:179–80; Crook, *North, South, and Powers*, 241, 251; Merli, *GB and Confederate Navy*, 114–15; Historicus letters in *Times*, 7, 8, 17 Nov. 1862 [letters reprinted in *Letters by Historicus on Some Questions of International*

Law (London, 1863), 3–15, 41–51]; E. D. Adams, *GB and Civil War,* 2:63; C. F. Adams, Jr., "Crisis of Foreign Intervention" 40–41; Lewis to Harcourt, 21 Nov. 1862, Harcourt Mss., box 12, Stanton-Harcourt Collection, Bodleian Lib., Oxford U. For his arguments pertaining to recognition and international law, Lewis cited John Austin, *The Province of Jurisprudence Determined* (London, 1832), 206–7; Emmerich de Vattel, *The Law of Nations, or, Principles of the Law of Nature Applied to the Conduct and Affairs of Nations and Sovereigns* (Philadelphia, 1817), book 3, sections 295–96; Wheaton, *Elements of International Law,* part 1, section 26.

38. Lewis, "Recognition of Independence."

39. Lord Napier (Brit. ambassador in St. Petersburg) to Russell, 8 Nov. 1862, cited in E. D. Adams, *GB and Civil War,* 2:63, 66; Lewis to Earl of Clarendon, 11 Nov. 1862, in Herbert Maxwell, *The Life and Letters of George William Frederick, Fourth Earl of Clarendon,* 2 vols. (London, 1913), 2:268; Jenkins, *Britain & War for Union,* 2:180; Lewis to Clarendon, 11 Nov. 1862, Clarendon Papers, Bodleian Lib.; Gladstone to wife, 12 Nov. 1862, cited in Morley, *Gladstone,* 2:85; Bright to Cobden, 24 Dec. 1862, Bright Papers, Brit. Lib., Add Mss., 43, 384, vol. 2; Henry Adams to C. F. Adams, Jr., 27 Jan. 1863, Worthington C. Ford, ed., *A Cycle of Adams Letters, 1861– 1865,* 2 vols. (Boston, 1920), 1:243–45; C. F. Adams Diary, 2, 13, 16, 17 Jan., 27 Feb. 1863, Adams Family Papers, Mass. Historical Society, Boston; C. F. Adams to Seward, 2 Jan. 1863, no. 289, Disp., GB (NA). See also Donaldson Jordan and Edwin J. Pratt, *Europe and the American Civil War* (Boston, 1931), 145–63. Russia did agree to give informal support to any Anglo-French effort that did not alienate the Union. This qualification was meaningless, since no one believed that the Union would lift the blockade.

40. For a prognostication on what would have happened to Anglo-American relations had England intervened in the Civil War, see Allan Nevins, *The War for the Union,* 4 vols. (New York, 1959–71), 2:242.

PRESSURE FROM WITHOUT

African Americans, British Public Opinion, and Civil War Diplomacy

★ ★ ★

R. J. M. BLACKETT

*W*riting in 1886, Samuel Fielden, one of the Haymarket Martyrs, reminisced of his youth in Todmorden in the 1850s about how his father would take him to political meetings where all the major issues affecting the British working class were discussed. Here, in the small textile town that straddles Lancashire and Yorkshire, young Fielden immersed himself in the heated debates about issues as far-reaching as factory reform and American slavery. This was the genesis of his radicalism. Of the many lectures and meetings he attended, none impressed him more than those at which American fugitive slaves, such as Henry "Box" Brown, spoke: "I went frequently to hear them describe the inhumanity of that horrible system, sometimes with my father, and at other times with my sister." The system's inhumanity and the fugitives' struggle to rid themselves of this oppression had a profound influence on Fielden, who remembered spending hours discussing the lectures with his playmates. The United States of America played a prominent part in all their lives: many of their families and friends had emigrated there, and those who stayed behind were employed in the textile industry, which relied almost exclusively on the southern states for its supply of cotton. When the Civil War disrupted the flow of cotton to Britain and threatened their livelihoods, there was what Fielden called "intense interest" among the people of Lancashire. They came together in Mechanics institutes and debating societies, town and church halls, and public places to discuss the causes and consequences of the war. During the summer months, "every night in the week there would be seen groups of men collected in the streets, and at the prominent corners discussing the latest news and forecasting the next, and in these groups there was always to be heard the advocates and champions of both sides."[1]

Textile workers' reactions to developments in the United States, Fielden insisted, were to a significant degree framed by the accounts that African Americans gave of their experiences as slaves and their encounters with racial discrimination. More importantly, these contacts, sustained over thirty years, provided a unique opportunity for wide-ranging discussions between the visitors and their hosts about the meaning and nature of oppression and about the best means to attain freedom. Periodically, African Americans and white American abolitionists ran into resistance from British workers who demanded that more attention be given to wage slavery at home than African slavery many miles away. Following a lecture by Henry Highland Garnet in 1851, a leader of the Tenant League in Ulster suggested that meaningful cooperation in the fight against oppression was only possible when Garnet and the Belfast Anti-Slavery Society, which had sponsored his visit, came to an appreciation of how existing landlord laws were used against tenants. But generally, a consensus emerged that this sort of international solidarity worked to the benefit of both slaves in the United States and workers seeking greater freedom in Britain.[2]

These antebellum contacts and the discussions that fueled them continued during the war. But the war altered the nature and conditions of the debate. What was once considered the highest expression of trans-Atlantic humanitarian solidarity ran the risk of being construed as foreign interference in the domestic affairs of the United States now that war had begun. But few thought seriously of severing the relationship. On the contrary, many believed that these contacts had to be strengthened if emancipation was to be achieved. Most historians of Anglo-American relations during the Civil War undervalue the extent and importance of these contacts. Donaldson Jordan and Edwin J. Pratt, in their path-breaking study of the period, said of African American contributions: "A number of escaped slaves, especially the former coachman of Jefferson Davis, were produced as lions at Unionist meetings; and the Reverend Sella Martin, a negro who received a parish in London, was one of the most effective of all the workers among the Dissenting bodies."[3]

I have identified almost forty African Americans in Britain who were actively engaged in the effort to win popular support for the Union. Some of them have virtually been forgotten by historians—such as J. H. Banks, a fugitive slave from Alabama who teamed up with J. W. C. Pennington for a series of lectures in Liverpool and Rhyl in early 1862. Other African American agitators in Britain during the war included William Howard Day, John Sella Martin, and Andrew Jackson, Davis's former coachman. Collectively these African Americans played a pivotal role in the effort to win popular support for the Union. We need to remember, however, as we consider their story, that these African Americans did not speak with one voice on all issues concerning the war. Early in the war, William Craft, long a critic of the United States government and influenced by Garrisonian views of the proslavery nature of the Constitution, insisted that war would never have occurred if the country had lived up to the principles of equality contained in the Declaration of Independence. Furthermore, he told a Sunderland audience, the North should allow the South to secede, for he was convinced that the Confederacy could not sustain itself with four million slaves in its midst.[4] Similarly, Day told a large public meeting of the African Aid Society in Birmingham in late 1861 that the war was a direct result of the arrogance of the "Anglo-Saxon races" who ignored the rights of Africans, and he condemned the Union for not abolishing all slave laws. Yet Day predicted that the slaves would be freed in two to three years, either as a consequence of America's heeding the word of God and doing what was right, or when the slaves united to take their freedom.[5]

African Americans and British abolitionists alike harbored considerable skepticism of Union intentions in the early months of the war. Martin ran into opposition from friends for this very reason. He could not convince George Thompson, the prominent British abolitionist and long an unflinching supporter of Garrisonian abolitionism, that Lincoln was seriously committed to abolition. As F. W. Chesson, Thompson's son-in-law and a prominent figure in the London Emancipation Committee, wrote in his diary, the "strongest fact that Mr. Martin appeared to be able to adduce was some remark which Mr. Lincoln had made to some member of the Seward family who had told it to somebody else, that somebody else repeating it to Mr. Martin!"[6] In spite of these differences, discussions of this sort and regular correspondence kept the lines of communication open between British and American abolitionists in this period of uncertainty. These differences were muted as the Lincoln government inched its way toward emancipation in 1862. By the end of the year, there was general unanimity among British abolitionists and African Americans in Britain about the need to support the cause of Union and emancipation.

British activists like Thompson who had been involved in the agitation for West Indian emancipation and who, since 1834, had continued to struggle for similar results in the United States, knew that success depended in large measure on popular support. Pressure from without had played a measurable role in pushing Parliament toward West Indian emancipation. And in the years since 1834, African Americans and white American abolitionists had used some of the same approaches in their appeals to the British public. They relied on this tradition as the effort to influence public opinion heated up following Lincoln's preliminary proclamation of emancipation in September 1862. African Americans lectured and held meetings in all parts of the country, in cities, towns, and villages.

Personal experience with slavery and discrimination lent poignancy to the message of these African American speakers. Jackson's lectures continued the prewar abolitionist tactic of telling about life as a slave and escape from bondage but added an assault on the Confederacy as the embodiment of slavery and criticism of the slaveholders' supporters in Britain. Of all the lecturers, he provided unique insights into the lives of Confederate leaders and life in Richmond, the Confederate capital. Here was a person who, by the standards of slavery, had a relatively comfortable position, yet nonetheless systematically plotted his escape: first, secretly learning to write so he could forge a pass that permitted him to travel out of Richmond; and second, making his way to Federal lines. One could question his assertion, while speaking in Britain, that there was little discrimination against blacks in the northern states. But audiences could never challenge his account of the horrors of slavery. Opponents of the Union breathed a sigh of relief when Jackson returned to the United States at the end of 1863. One insisted that the pro-Union forces had lost their main weapon in the battle to win public opinion. "They have ceased to command an audience in Lancashire now that President Davis's mythical ex-coachman (who was really worth seeing and listening to) is no longer available for diversifying the humdrum of an anti-slavery speech with a racy natural joke worth all the money."[7]

Throughout the war, African Americans had a profound influence on the direction of British public debate about the Civil War. Undoubtedly, part of their success was due to the enormous impact of the United States on the lives of many in Britain. Even if one was not a textile worker whose livelihood depended on the continued supply of southern cotton, one might be affected by the relevance of the American political system to the continuing debate over political reform in Britain. For many of those without the vote, "Americanization" and "democratization," as Henry Pilling points out, were almost synonymous conceptions. British liberals found inspiration in the American example. For conservatives in Britain, especially those of the upper class, on the other hand, the United States connoted the vulgarization of political and social life. Democracy, they insisted, led to mediocrity, for it discouraged the best men from becoming involved.[8]

Direct ties of a more personal nature also focused British attention on American affairs. By 1860, many people in Britain had relations in, or knew of someone who had immigrated to, the United States in search of better opportunities. For some, letters from family members in America brought the sad news of the death of relations and friends in the Civil War's battles. News of the war was eagerly awaited throughout Great Britain. Battle reports were read and maps consulted to pinpoint the locations of the war's contests. The diary of John Ward, a weaver from Low Moor, contains many entries about his regular hikes to Clitheroe to read newspaper accounts of the war and political developments in America. At Stalybridge, telegrams from the United States were posted at the Mechanics Institute and attracted large crowds. Lecturers drew on a common frame of reference when they talked about the Civil War. Therefore we should not be surprised that thousands throughout Great Britain attended lectures and meetings concerned with British policies toward the Civil War. An estimated ten thousand people attended an open-air meeting in the market place at Ashton to hear opposing sides debate the British position on the war.[9] British interest in the war was intense.

The working people who attended these lectures and meetings were well informed about developments in America. Many, particularly in the textile towns, were affected directly by the war's impact on the supply of cotton. In 1860 there were close to two thousand cotton factories employing one-half million operatives in Lancashire and neighboring counties. An estimated four million of the country's population of twenty-one million were dependent on the industry. Significant percentages of the population of Lancashire and Cheshire cotton towns were employed in the industry: Blackburn, 34 percent; Preston, 30 percent; Oldham, 29 percent; Bolton, 24 percent; Stockport, 34 percent; Ashton, 31 percent; and Stalybridge, 41 percent.[10] These and other cotton towns were immediately affected by the dramatic fall in the supply of cotton from America brought on by the war. Thousands were idled when factories closed their doors or were forced to revert to short time, and there were widespread concerns that economic dislocation could lead to political unrest.

It is not surprising that these developments had a profound effect on British public opinion. In September 1861, Henry Lord, the U.S. consul in Manchester, wrote Union secretary of state William H. Seward that public sentiment in the town was "almost unanimously adverse" to the Northern cause.[11] The British government's early recognition of the Confederacy as a belligerent, its declaration of neutrality, periodic calls in Parliament by Confederate supporters for rejecting the Union blockade of southern ports as a violation of international law, and their frequent efforts to win recognition for the South suggested to many the likelihood that, sooner or later, the government would have to reconsider its policy of neutrality. This possibility seemed even more imminent at the end of 1861 when a Union naval officer seized two Confederate commissioners, James Mason and John Slidell, from the British ship *Trent* while they were on their way to Britain. The British government demanded the prompt release of the commissioners, insisted on adequate reparations from Washington, and made preparations for war should the Union government reject these demands. Slow communications between the two countries provided an opportunity for cooler heads to prevail, and the release of the commissioners dispersed the war clouds. But the "*Trent* Affair" and the passions it unleashed on both sides of the Atlantic confirmed the unpredictability and fluidity of the relationship between Washington and London.

It is that atmosphere of uncertainty which forms the backdrop to this examination of how the working class reacted to the Civil War and of the efforts that were made to rally public opinion as a way of influencing government policy. This approach differs fundamentally from those studies which have traditionally examined events from the vantage point of the twentieth century, secure in the knowledge that the Palmerston government, while tempted at times, never seriously considered deviating from its policy of neutrality. My intention in this essay, in contrast, is to look at how public reactions to developments in America evolved; how local and national organizations attempted to frame and influence the nature of that reaction; and finally, what attempts were made to influence government policy in a period when few were convinced that the government's policies were immutable. Some contemporaries did contend that working-class pressure made the difference in warding off British recognition of the Confederacy. Months after the successful pro-Union meeting organized by the London trade unionists and the London Emancipation Society, an editor of a major labor newspaper insisted that it had a "considerable influence in shaping the after-policy of the English

Cabinet on the American Question." No evidence was provided to support such a serious claim, but, then, no evidence was needed. Melvin Small has suggested one approach that, on the face of it, could provide some answers. He has argued that while public opinion can limit options, it is impossible to prove that it ever influences policy. Jordan and Pratt seem to agree. They have called working-class influence on government policy during this period a "dead weight," one that limited the government's freedom to act on any issue that the class opposed.[12] Yet there is no credible evidence that public opinion in this period either limited government options or directly influenced policy. Rather, the documentary record shows (and what seems to me to be of more historical interest) an almost universally accepted conviction that government policy was susceptible to public pressure and that for this very reason individuals were obligated to become involved in the effort to marshal public opinion in support of the causes in which they believed.

It is generally accepted that in order for agitators to gain public approval for a given position, their issues must be framed in ways that address the most pressing needs of the community. All of this assumes that one is not tilling barren ground, that local events, whether economic, social, or political, make the community partial to one's views. That requires a dialogue between the community and those seeking to win its approval.

In the case of the Civil War, the British government's initial declaration of neutrality significantly framed how the issues were presented. It forced Confederate supporters into the position of demanding changes in a policy that, by and large, seemed to be serving the country well. Their opponents simply had to show that there was no popular support for change. Confederate supporters found themselves in the disadvantageous position of having to present a united front, or if that were not possible, at least to demonstrate that their sustained agitation represented, in some way, a public endorsement of the call for change. This is why they placed so much emphasis on the need to coordinate public expressions of approval with motions in Parliament calling for a change in government policy. When, for example, word of Union general Joe Hooker's defeat at Chancellorsville arrived in May 1863, James Spence of Liverpool, the major figure in the pro-Confederate movement, and the leaders of the Southern lobby arranged a series of public meetings in the weeks before motions calling for recognition of the Confederacy were to be submitted in both the House of Lords and Commons.[13]

What pro-Union and pro-Confederate activists had in common was their shared belief that governments could be forced to act if organized and sustained public pressure were brought to bear on them. Past experience spoke to the efficacy of this approach. West Indian emancipation had been the result of a sustained public agitation almost thirty years before, and the despised Corn Laws were repealed as a result of a similar campaign. "If Preston, and Manchester, and Bolton, and Leeds, and Birmingham, and London, and such like places press the government," Joseph Barker, a Confederate supporter, declared, "then they will feel at liberty" to recognize the Confederacy. The trick, especially for southern sympathizers, was to make sure that public opinion delivered a clear message. J. L. Quarmby, secretary of the Oldham branch of the Southern Independence Association, while admitting the importance of remonstrances from major cities, recognized that it would take a united voice to move British policy. "Public opinion here [in Mossley] is divided upon the question of North and South and the government which is a reflex of it, is consequently powerless—its wheels are clogged."[14]

Mossley, like other towns and cities, never spoke with a united voice because it was contested ground. Neither side gave much quarter. When, in April 1863, the old Preston Anti-Slavery Society, which was affiliated with the British and Foreign Anti-Slavery Society, organized a successful meeting at which George Thompson, Union agent Peter Sinclair, and others spoke, and at which unanimous resolutions in support of the Union and emancipation were adopted, local Confederate sympathizers sprang into action. The meeting, "A Believer in the South" wrote, was an attempt to give a false impression that the people of Preston supported the Union. Within two months, friends of the Confederacy announced the formation of the Preston Southern Club, with membership open to manufacturers, merchants, tradesmen, and artisans, its aim to counter and defeat any attempts to drum up public support for the Union. The club's first meeting, planned for late June, was addressed by a delegation from Manchester and adopted resolutions in support of John Roebuck's motion in the House of Commons regarding recognition of the Confederacy. Meetings of this sort, a local editor observed, were meant not only to "develop but foster public opinion, while they at the same time annihilate popular errors." He predicted the "final triumph of those who advocate recognition . . . now that public opinion is so openly and honestly expressed." His confidence, however, proved premature. Within weeks, opponents of the Southern Club met to form a local branch of the Union and Emancipation Society.[15] Mossley continued to speak with two voices.

Lecturers were constantly challenged, and while it appears that these challenges were spontaneous expressions of opposition, they were frequently organized, vociferous, and mean-spirited. Heckling, which had been raised to an art form, sometimes took unusual twists. At one public meeting, opponents of a speaker rose to their feet, swaying and waving their arms and moving in circles. Their antics were so well orchestrated that they could not have been spontaneous. Heckling and challenges of this sort sometimes spilled over into violence. The near-riot that occurred at a pro-Union meeting in Bristol in late 1864 was unusual, but there were many occasions when people were punched or generally manhandled. When opponents of the Confederacy thought that John Matthews had crossed the bounds of decency in his insults of a fugitive slave during an open-air lecture at Stalybridge, they threatened to throw him in the canal and would have done so had he not been rescued by friends.[16]

To reach and inform the public and discuss issues across the country, pro-Union and pro-Confederate advocates required well-organized propaganda machines. Both sides in the dispute perfected such organizations by late 1862. Pro-Union forces had something of a head start, as they were able to draw on the abolitionist societies that had survived into the 1850s. Although both the British and Foreign Anti-Slavery Society (BFASS) and the London Emancipation Committee (LEC) had lost some of their sting and enthusiasm by the outbreak of the war, their machinery was nonetheless in place and could be reactivated once the decision was made to take the message to the people. Their task was made easier by the survival of a number of provincial auxiliaries. The LEC was reorganized in late 1862 as the London Emancipation Society (LES), with many of the same leaders, including Thompson and Chesson. The BFASS was much slower to move, largely because many of its leaders were peace advocates and so could not bring themselves to endorse a war, but also because a few of them genuinely distrusted Union intentions. Martin was so frustrated by this inactivity that he dubbed the society an "antiquated affair, the members of which met but once a year for the purpose of instituting deputations, that did nothing but sprinkle rose water on the feet of a few conservative lords." The LES and the BFASS were joined in early 1863 by the Manchester Union and Emancipation Society, formed expressly for the purpose of agitating the issues in the north of England.[17]

Confederate supporters were not slow to act. Although they formed no major national organization until mid-1863, local Southern Clubs took responsibility for getting the message out to their communities. Not surprisingly, given Liverpool's extensive trading contacts with the southern states, the first of these clubs was formed in that city in September 1862, largely due to Spence's efforts. Unlike clubs that formed later, the Liverpool group represented more than just an arm of Confederate propaganda. It was also a traditional club with a committee to regulate the price of wines and a membership fee well beyond the reach of the average Liverpudlian. Its executive committee consisted of leaders of some of the major city firms doing business in the South. Late in 1862, friends of the Confederacy in London formed the Confederate Aid Association (CAA). A rather ephemeral organization, the association seems to have been run by Rector Smith, a medical doctor from Kentucky with a practice in London; and Alexander Beresford Hope, a substantial landowner in Kent and one of the leading figures in the Confederate cause.[18] While the CAA directed most of its efforts to influencing members of Parliament, the Southern Independence Association (SIA), formed in Manchester in late May 1863, aimed to combine lobbying activities on the national level with efforts at the local level. Another pro-Confederate society, but one with much less public visibility, was the Society to Promote the Cessation of Hostilities in America. This group, an apparent successor to the CAA, formed in the fall of 1863 and claimed a membership of 5,000 nine months later. Confederate agent Matthew Maury seems to have financed most of its activities.[19]

All these organizations relied on a combination of lecturers, public meetings, pamphlets, fact sheets, placards, and handbills to get their messages across. Both sides put considerable stock in public meetings and lectures as the best means of reaching the public. Sinclair claimed to have held seventy meetings in the first months of 1863, and Jackson seems to have held at least that many. Barker; Rev. E. A. Verity, vicar at Habergam Eaves, near Burnley; T. B. Kershaw (a mill manager at Manchester); and J. H. Smith may have given as many, but it is more difficult to determine the number with any precision. While the Confederate lecturers generally worked alone, their Union counterparts frequently worked in pairs: Martin and Thompson; Jackson and Thompson; Martin and Washington Wilkes; and T. Morris Chester (an African American who in 1864 became a war correspondent for the *Philadelphia Press*) and Frederick Tomkins, the London barrister, just to mention a few.[20] Lectures and meetings were widely advertised with placards and posters. Some even complained that these posters were becoming an eyesore. Lord reported that the SIA displayed posters, measuring one by one and one-half yards, throughout the city. Proclaiming "The Hypocrisy of the North on Slavery," the poster quoted Seward as having said that slavery was no longer an issue in the war. The following day, the Union and Emancipation Society countered with a similarly sized poster headed "Lying Versus So Called Hypocrisy," showing that Seward's words had been taken out of context.[21]

Short, pithy fact sheets—or, as the SIA called them, "Papers for the People"—carried an important part of the propaganda effort. The SIA claimed to have issued 85,000 of these papers, circulated 160,000 handbills, and printed 10,000 placards and reports of speeches in the first six months of its existence. Chesson reported a similar approach by the LES. Within the first two months of its existence, the LES had arranged a number of meetings in and around London, sent circulars to clergy and ministers asking them to speak on emancipation at New Year's service, printed and circulated thousands of copies of tracts, and sent weekly fact sheets with information on emancipation to more than three hundred newspapers.[22]

Local supporters provided the oil that greased this extensive and sometimes very sophisticated national propaganda machine. It was these people who first got together to discuss the Civil War and its impact on their lives, and it was at the local level that decisions were made about what actions should be taken. Local supporters took on the major responsibility for collecting signatures on petitions to Parliament and the government and proved to be the national organizations' most valuable asset.

An examination of one area—in this case the Ashton and Stalybridge area—may help us piece together the way local conditions, local leadership, and national organizations came together in an effort to give expression to public opinion and influence government policy. As we have seen, Ashton, like all the other textile towns across the country, was heavily dependent on American cotton. The outbreak of hostilities in America, which threatened the supply of cotton, produced considerable anxiety among those who worked in the mills. Although in the early months of the war stockpiles of cotton were enough to offset the drop in supply, many textile communities began to feel the pinch almost immediately. By early 1862, there were unmistakable signs that the Cotton Famine was taking hold. Only 40 of the 188 mills in Ashton and Stalybridge, employing 8,144 of 66,527 operatives, were working full-time in April. Ashton's pauperism rate in June 1861 was 1.3 percent of a population of 134,761, the lowest rate in England; by June 1862, it had risen to 6.4 percent. The effect of the famine, measured by the number of cotton operatives on relief, peaked in the last two months of 1862. In Ashton there were 57,000 on relief, the highest number in Lancashire and Cheshire.[23]

The famine cut a broad swath of devastation in every cotton town. Joseph Peacock, secretary of the Padiham Operative Relief Committee, observed that "crowds of unemployed men, women and children throng the streets and thoroughfares, with haggard looks and sunken eyes, which betoken hearts fast setting down into despair."[24] What were operatives to do? For many, relief was a last resort. They found the labor tests and other means of determining the level of relief degrading. Many textile workers sold their possessions and moved in with relatives before they could bring themselves to ask for relief. Some advocated emigration to either the United States or a British colony as the most effective way of dealing with the sudden rise in unemployment. Others demanded that the government do all within its power to encourage the cultivation of cotton in British colonies, especially in India, as the best means of undermining the American monopoly.

Two public meetings in Ashton in early March 1862 condemned labor tests and explored ways of procuring an alternative supply of cotton. But a group of dissenters insisted that increasing the supply of cotton from India was a long-term proposition that did absolutely nothing to address the immediate needs of those who were out of work. Here was a situation, they insisted, where the economic life of the community was being affected by political decisions made thousands of miles away. This problem had to be solved, therefore, in the political arena. Only the government's recognition of the Confederacy could ensure an adequate and immediate supply of cotton. But Ashton, like many English communities, was not of one mind on the American situation. Many residents believed that recognition of the Confederacy would violate Great Britain's abolitionist traditions. How could a country that had long prided itself on being in the forefront of the struggle against slavery recognize a nation whose vice president had declared that its cornerstone was slavery? Furthermore, some people in Ashton also feared that recognition would lead to war with the Union.

Given these constraints, proponents of recognition in Ashton had to be circumspect. Placards issued by a committee of employers and employed announced a meeting for 30 April to discuss unemployment and the fear of impending starvation rather than specifying that the proposed gathering was designed to support recognition of the Confederacy. But even such cautious tactics encountered resistance. Interpreting the call as a subterfuge, Union supporters posted placards warning the town that the organizers planned to use concerns for the operatives' future as a device to win approval for recognition of the Confederacy. One such placard, issued by a "Committee of Working Men" dedicated to "peace, protection of labour, property, and the liberty of mankind, irrespective of rank or condition, country or colour," claimed that the organizers of the meeting were hirelings of Confederate agents. It is impossible to determine if all of the meeting's organizing committee were in the pay of Confederate agents, but money to finance and promote the meeting did come from that source. The leading figure among the organizers was William Aitken. An old Chartist,[25] Aitken had earlier spent some time in prison for his activities. After his release, he emigrated to the United States, where he lived a number of years before returning to England. He was an early advocate of southern independence.[26]

Divisions within Ashton precluded anything substantive from coming out of the meeting. In his opening speech, Aitken insisted that working people were the innocent victims of a war in which Americans—whom he likened to Goths and Vandals—were "hacking each other to pieces and destroying their country" and inflicting suffering on innocent textile workers. The only practical solution was to pressure the government to recognize the South. Matthews put it more directly: If, as he was convinced, recognition was inevitable, why delay and encourage so much suffering among an innocent people? Before the motion calling for recognition could be moved, however, a John Johnson submitted an amendment that condemned southern slavery and called on the government to join the Union in the effort to crush a revolt against "the most liberal government in the world." Confusion followed, and it seemed that the large crowd, unable to hear what was being proposed, voted in support of both the amendment and the motion! Ashton remained contested ground. Four weeks later, at a meeting called to petition the government to invest in expanding the infrastructure of India so as to facilitate the export of cotton, and to encourage cultivation in other British colonies, James Nield of Mossley insisted that the unemployed could not wait and that their needs could be met if the South were recognized. His motion for recognition was defeated by an amendment that insisted, in part, that the time was not ripe for recognition. The public debate continued on Stalybridge's

Plantation Ground in August, when Jacob Green, a fugitive slave, accused a number of local people of being in the pay of the South. Matthews dismissed Green's claim and insisted that the Union was a slaveholding government and that both the Union and the British government had supported slavery by buying slave-grown goods.[27]

The drive for recognition originated as the work of a small group of local people motivated by a commitment to find a reasonably quick solution to rising economic problems. Aitkin, Matthews, and others had been discussing these issues for some time. Similar concerns were being aired in other parts of Lancashire and Cheshire, and similar solutions proposed. But Green was also right: agents of the Confederacy had stepped in to support and give some direction to these local efforts. Confederate agents decided sometime early in 1862 to make every effort to rally public support behind the call for either mediation of the Civil War or recognition of the Confederacy. Henry Hotze, the Confederacy's chief propaganda agent in England, reported home at the time about his plans to use one thousand pounds for a public campaign in the hardest-hit areas of Britain. And Spence informed Mason that a deputation of working men in the cotton trade had visited him in Liverpool at the end of April. They were beginning to feel the pinch and wanted to act. Spence suggested that they call meetings throughout the district and draw up petitions to Parliament calling for recognition of the Confederacy as a way to end the war. Spence also gave them money to help with the expenses of organizing the meetings and promised continued support. He even offered to help draw up the petitions.[28]

The pro-Confederates apparently included, besides Aitkin and Matthews, Mortimer Grimshaw, an old Chartist from Blackburn who, during labor unrest in the late fifties, had gained a reputation as an active opponent of strikes and an agent of factory owners. The group held a series of organizational meetings at Stockport, Bollington, Blackburn, Ashton, and other towns at which delegates were to be selected to a major meeting in Bolton in July. The expressed purpose of the organizational meetings in Blackburn, "One of the Delegates" wrote to a local newspaper, was to galvanize working-class opinion in favor of a motion pending before Parliament by John Turner Hopwood, member of Parliament for Clitheroe, calling on the government to offer to mediate the Civil War. But an amendment insisting that the government do all it could to persuade the southern rebels to return to the Union was carried overwhelmingly, and Hopwood was condemned for encouraging interference in another country while opposing extension of the franchise to working people at home. The meeting closed with a vote of no confidence in the organizers. Within days of this defeat, a few prominent local Confederate supporters requested that the mayor call a meeting to examine all the issues. It was rumored that some of the mill owners had promised to send their workers to the meeting. But here, too, the organizers ran into problems: although a motion condemning meddlesome interference in the affairs of another country failed for want of a seconder, the meeting adopted a compromise motion that endorsed, as a general principle, the need for all disputes to be submitted to arbitration.[29]

These were hardly the results that organizers had anticipated. If Quarmby was right, public opinion could only be influential if it spoke with a united voice. Yet public opinion had sent mixed messages, and this continued to be the case when twenty-three delegates from across the two counties most affected by the cotton shortage met in convention at Bolton in July. James Hardy, one of those who opposed the meeting's decision to petition the government in favor of recognition, reported that delegates divided almost equally on all of the major issues discussed, and he condemned the organizers, particularly Grimshaw, for bringing in drunk men "who represent no class of operatives," in an effort to carry the vote. Thomas Evans, a delegate from Manchester, moved an amendment which stated that the time was not right for arbitration and that the government ought to be directing its efforts to promoting the expansion of cotton cultivation in India as the best way to alleviate the country's almost total reliance on American cotton. In the end, the pro-Confederate forces had their way, but only by the narrowest of margins.[30]

There was a general consensus, even among southerners in Britain, that local opposition had undermined the objective of these meetings. Hotze thought that while the "intelligent classes" were with the Confederacy, they were having a difficult time winning support among the working class. Lancashire operatives, he wrote Confederate secretary of state Judah Benjamin, were "actively inimical," for they had an "instinctive aversion" to slavery. Their patience and long-suffering during the Cotton Famine stemmed from "a consciousness" that to act otherwise would promote slavery.[31]

Brian Jenkins suggests a link between the failure of the Blackburn meeting and Palmerston's rejection in the Commons of a call for recognition.[32] He may well be right. Given the government's policy of neutrality, the ebb and flow of the war, and the uncertainty about the consequences of recognition, it was enough for Union sympathizers to show that the public was deeply divided to undermine the campaign for recognition. The demands on Confederate sympathizers were different and more formidable: they had the nearly impossible task of showing a public united in the conviction that it was in the best interest of the country to recognize the rebels.

In spite of this initial failure, Confederate sympathizers had no alternative but to keep agitating the issues in public in the hope that the continuing crisis in the cotton industry and a possible turn in the tide of the war would galvanize public opinion in their favor. Spence saw these links and the demands they imposed on Confederate supporters. The war, he insisted in late 1863, could not be won without foreign intervention, and the only power that could move the government to act was pressure from the public. With this in mind, he organized a series of public meetings. There were more than four thousand people at a Glasgow gathering, and the meeting voted up a series of resolutions in favor of the Confederacy, in spite of the presence of one thousand opponents. But if Spence's spirits were temporarily buoyed by the reception he received at these meetings, the opposition gave him no quarter. In letters to the press, Martin offered a point-by-point refutation of Spence's claims. Having sown the wind, he wrote, the Confederacy was now reaping the whirlwind. "Governing their plantations by the revolver and the poor whites by the bowie-knife, what is more natural than that the Southerners should melt the private revolver into the cannon of the public battlefield, and beat their bowie-knifes into swords of rebellion[?]" Martin traveled to Glasgow to undermine any advantage that Spence may have gained. Although anti-Union forces made life difficult for him, in the end, the meeting voted in favor of the Union and emancipation. While Spence may have smiled derisively at Martin's discomfort, such sustained and organized opposition did nothing to help the Confederate cause.[33] Spence did win the endorsements of the meetings that his local supporters organized, but as he himself admitted, the opposition gave him, and all other pro-Confederate lecturers, little quarter.

While the effort to win working-class support for the South in the summer of 1862 fell far short of the mark, it did result in the formation of a number of local Southern Clubs that in mid-1863 came together as affiliates of the Southern Independence Association. It is difficult to determine the size and the class composition of these clubs. William Bell, an old Chartist from Haywood and an opponent of the South, observed that members of the clubs were a "curious compound of political opinion. . . . The high-bred aristocrat, who has taken every opportunity to oppose the spread of liberal opinions, and the rich manufacturer, who has become known to the public through his advocacy of those opinions." Bell was only partially right; there were, for instance, a number of working people, particularly skilled laborers, who were members of clubs like the one in Stalybridge, which was formed in September 1862. But working people seem to have played a greater leadership role in local Union and Emancipation societies. The Ashton branch, for instance, was made up almost entirely of working men.[34]

It is these societies that were responsible for organizing public meetings and countering the activities of the opposition. In late February 1863, pro-Union organizers brought Thompson to Ashton for a large public meeting attended mainly by the working class. The following week a group of working men arranged a meeting addressed by Jackson and Sinclair. In May, pro-Confederate supporters countered with Barker, who ran into stiff opposition, not so much because of his views on the war but because his habit of changing sides in disputes made him untrustworthy. Barker could not win a vote of confidence in Ashton, and while resolutions of support for the South were passed in Stalybridge, the meeting was not well attended. These were immediately followed by an open-air meeting on the Plantation Ground attended by "several hundred" who condemned Barker's views.[35] Barker had much more success elsewhere and carried a number of meetings before he promptly, but not surprisingly, gave up his active promotion of the Confederacy for other causes.

The debate in Ashton, Stalybridge, and elsewhere continued for the rest of the war. In the summer of 1864, Confederate supporters seem to have decided on a different approach. Attempts to win working-class support had not been uniformly successful. So southern sympathizers looked to other quarters for support. At an Ashton meeting held three days before William Lindsay's motion in the House of Commons calling for recognition, according to one speaker, there were none of the familiar working-class faces. Although there were a few workers present, the Reverend F. H. Williams made a point of emphasizing that this was a "meeting of the respectable inhabitants—the male inhabitants of Ashton."[36]

Allied with Lindsay's motion was an effort by Confederate sympathizers to organize a massive petition campaign in favor of the South. Two petitions were organized, one by the Society to Promote the Cessation of Hostilities in America and paid for by Maury, the other by the SIA. Ostensibly, the drive was meant to demonstrate the extent of public support for peace in America, but there was no doubt that its real intent was to show the depth of support for the Confederacy. Meetings were held in thirty towns in Lancashire in the months leading up to submission of the petitions to Parliament in July. Canvassers, some of whom were paid as much as four shillings per day, went door to door and stood outside mill gates collecting signatures. Petitions were placed in cotton mills, and, as the *Index* proudly reported, "every respectable mill-owner or other capitalist who is largely an employer of labour, is offering all reasonable facilities for carrying out this important measure." Opponents accused the organizers of collecting signatures under false pretenses by using the plea of "full time" and "good cotton" on a petition that called for southern independence.[37]

The petition to the House of Commons contained sixty thousand names, including "the whole list of mercantile and manufacturing firms that have done most towards making Manchester the commercial metropolis of these counties." A deputation of working men that met with Foreign Secretary Lord John Russell carried a memorial signed by an estimated ninety thousand operatives calling on the government to enter into discussions with European powers on the best way to end the war. While there had only been fifteen petitions from both sides in 1863, most of them submitted to coincide with Roebuck's failed motion for recognition in midsummer, the number of petitions increased dramatically in 1864. There were at least eighty-one organized by one or another of the pro-Confederate groups. Three of them called for peace and southern independence, and seventy-eight for termination of the war. About twenty-four of the latter came from Ireland, reflecting the recent attempts by Hotze and other Confederate agents to staunch the flow of Irish immigrants to the North. Of the seventy-eight petitions calling for termination of the war, ten came from towns so small that they are not on a modern road map; twenty-four were from small towns and villages; twelve were from London; and six were from Lancashire and Cheshire. There were only eighteen petitions from the Union and Emancipation Society, the majority of them from either cities or cotton towns.[38] Obviously, Spence's dictum provided the driving force behind the Confederate barrage of petitions: southern supporters felt that public opinion provided the only way to trigger the intervention of foreign powers in the Civil War.

Yet there is something plaintive in the lament of J. Whitehead, a member of the Oldham SIA, that the association could have been more effective had it started its petition drive earlier.[39] Whitehead's lament was simply a poignant expression of the dilemma that Spence identified. Few—and Whitehead was not one of them—believed that the British government was unalterably committed to its policy of neutrality. If the Confederacy was not to be recognized, why, many outside the government asked, was Palmerston meeting with Mason in the summer of 1864? When Spence wrote Mason encouraging him to return to London from Paris for the meeting, he observed that the prime minister was "tending in our favor yet hesitating and unsettled." Spence may have lost all sense of reality, but his apparent optimism was born of the conviction that southern independence could still be assured if public pressure forced the government to alter its policy. Some on the Union side, in spite of the changing tide of war and Lincoln's reelection in late 1864, were still not convinced that their government had abandoned all plans for interfering in the war. It was not until Union forces captured Fort Fisher, the gateway to the Cape Fear River and Wilmington, North Carolina, in January 1865 that Freeman Morse could bring himself to declare that such an outcome was no longer possible. It is this uncertainty which sustained for so long what Jordan and Pratt have called the "mirage of recognition" among Confederate supporters in Britain.[40]

In the end, we need to ask why anyone believed that the British government would intervene in the Civil War during a period of relative prosperity. The famine may have devastated the cotton districts, but the period 1860 to 1866 was one of general prosperity, a period during which the value of exports and imports rose, government expenditures fell, taxes were lowered, and duties were reduced on tea and sugar. But all eyes were indeed fixed on the cotton district; many expected that the famine would produce political unrest. The operatives of these towns had an active political and social agenda: they called for increased support for emigration; demanded that government encourage the cultivation of cotton in India and other British colonies; and, at least in the case of Confederate sympathizers, called on the government to intervene either to stop the war or recognize the South. Such an active political agenda does not fit Frank Owsley's description of the cotton operative as "politically apathetic, sodden, ignorant, and docile with the exception of a few intelligent and earnest leaders."[41] They were nothing of the kind.

Black Americans played a pivotal role in the British public debate over the war. Theirs was a presence that could not be ignored, and their frequent visits to the cotton districts helped many of those suffering from the effects of the famine to focus on the larger struggle against oppression. Not everyone saw it this way. All of these black Americans were placed in the uncomfortable position of having to explain their support for a nation that discriminated against them and refused to grant them any of the rights enjoyed by white citizens. The question cut to the heart of the American paradox, and African Americans were hard pressed to offer acceptable explanations for this failure. Declarations about perceptible improvements in the North had a hollow ring to them. But there was no doubt that the Union had moved aggressively against slavery, while the Confederacy continued to insist that its institutions were not a fit subject for debate even among friends.

The link between British working-class political aspirations, the activities of black Americans, and the image of the United States as the embodiment of democratic aspirations continued to be a potent force in the struggle for political reform in Britain long after the war. It may have had its most poignant expression in a large franchise meeting in Kilmarnock, Scotland, in 1884. The organizers decorated the platform with a flag of 1831 on which were embroidered the words "Reform, good laws, cheap government" and with the Stars and Stripes, a gift from Lincoln to the people of the small weaving town of Newmilns twenty years before. The flag, local lore has it, was presented to the people of Newmilns by John Brooks, a black American living in Glasgow.[42]

QUESTION: You emphasize time and again the Cotton Famine. Howard Jones indicated that it was not all that severe, that there was a huge cotton surplus because just before the war there were a couple of bumper crops, and because the Union was able to ship some cotton when its armies captured some southern towns. Was he wrong? Or is there some compromise position here?

ANSWER: There was a surplus of cotton in the early part of the war that postponed the impact of the famine. But very early on, in anticipation of that famine, manufacturers and spinners began to speculate in cotton, and this removed a lot of cotton from the market. So, slowly, economic dislocations were caused by the shortage of cotton. By the end of 1862, the major cotton towns, which relied heavily on southern cotton, were feeling the pinch. Gladstone and others were painting a rosy picture of the economy. They were correct in the national scope of things. But authorities worried that areas of England which long had a tradition of rebellion, particularly during the Chartist period of the 1830s and 1840s, would rise up once again if the cotton scarcity became too severe. So yes, the Cotton Famine was not severe in the early part of the war. But in 1864, Ashton still had 16 percent unemployment. And Ashton, for instance, at the height of the famine, had 41 percent of its working population unemployed.

QUESTION: How high on the political agenda of Great Britain was this issue of recognition as compared to other issues affecting that country at the same time?

ANSWER: It was very high because there were so many things associated with it. The issue of alternative supplies of cotton became critical. There was a lot of political agitation, for instance, to get the British government to improve the infrastructure of India so that more cotton could be produced there and shipped to England. Why, people were asking, had these cotton manufacturers taken so long to develop alternative supplies of the material, given the American monopoly on cotton? This issue raised domestic political debate to a higher intensity.

The Civil War stirred all sorts of class interests in British society. Until at least 1884, and well into later battles over political reform in Britain, the issue of America as symbol would remain important. People related the American Civil War to a number of domestic political issues, mainly the extension of the vote, which was the dominant issue in this period. We can learn a lot about domestic political differences in Britain by looking at how the working classes reacted to the assassination of Lincoln.

QUESTION: Did those in Great Britain who supported the Confederacy have more of a stake in the cotton industry? Were they the managers and owners of the factories?

ANSWER: It is hard to tell. A lot of evidence seems to support the idea that many of the owners supported the Confederacy. But then there were a number of important owners who did not support the Confederacy. I think that local politics had more to do with it: mill owners who tended to vote Conservative were more sympathetic with the Confederacy than those who supported the Liberals—and I don't mean that term with small letters. I am referring to political parties. Although there were owners of large mills who were both Liberal and supported the Confederacy, I have not identified Conservative mill owners who supported the Union. There were some Conservatives who were opposed to both the Union and the Confederacy. They objected to the Union for its vulgarization of politics. The Union seemed to be the embodiment of all the worst things that you could see in any civilized society. Its voters elected people who were incompetent and did not have the best interests of society in mind. How could any civilized people elect a rail splitter as president? It's just not done! These Conservatives also objected to the Confederacy because any act of rebellion would be interpreted by them as a dangerous attack on constituted authority. That is the one ground on which Conservatives—Tories—could be critical of the Confederacy. That's not how you do things! Things are done in a constitutional way.

QUESTION: Given that slavery was both an economic and a moral issue, how did pro-Union people in Great Britain address the concerns about unemployment caused by the shortage of Southern cotton?

ANSWER: In a number of indirect ways. Obviously, they can address the question by saying, "We had cotton flowing in here all the time until these foolish people in the South decided to rebel." But what really sank the Confederacy in the eyes of many was when, after the fall of New Orleans, they decided to burn cotton there so that it would not fall into Union hands. The Confederacy had been arguing all along that "Cotton was King" and that the lack of cotton could dethrone the monarchy in Britain. The active destruction of the cotton crop so that it could not get over to Lancashire was enough to ruin the Confederate image in many eyes. The British could also say, "What would you expect of people who are slaveholders, anyway? They do these sorts of intemperate things." So they could mix the moral issues with the question of the supply of cotton.

QUESTION: Do you know of any attempts by Confederate leaders to send slaves to Great Britain to counter the propaganda of fugitive slaves who were speaking out on behalf of the North, or did southerners stick exclusively to the issue of cotton?

ANSWER: No, they didn't enlist the help of slaves in the propaganda effort. It would have been just too bizarre.

I should point out that sometimes Confederate agents in Britain had problems dealing with the statements of their supporters as well as with those of their antagonists. To rally enthusiasm for the South, British sympathizers were in the habit of claiming that ultimately the Confederacy would have to emancipate the slaves. There was no British Confederate sympathizer that I know of who did not make this argument. All the while, Confederate agents kept telling their British sympathizers to stop such prognoses. "We cannot negotiate slavery. It is not up for discussion," they said. What the Confederate agents were willing to do was float the idea that the Confederacy intended to arm a number of its slaves on the promise of freedom—that they would put fifty thousand slaves in gray uniforms and give them their liberty when the war was over. This proposal briefly caused concern among pro-Union people in Britain, particularly fugitive slaves. But they soon answered it: they dared the South to do it. For instance, one of them wrote a letter to one of the major newspapers in London saying that if the Confederates tried the scheme, they had better keep those slaves on the front lines, or the slaves would take the opportunity to shoot Confederate soldiers. The proposal to arm the slaves was a desperate ploy on the part of Confederate agents to win some points on the moral issue of abolition, but they could not really do it because their whole society, after all, was based on slavery.

QUESTION: Howard Jones suggested that Confederate propaganda emphasized that Lincoln's Emancipation Proclamation would stir up a servile insurrection. Was this effective propaganda?

ANSWER: To an extent, it was a red herring. After all, by a couple of months after the Emancipation Proclamation, it was clear that the predicted slave insurrection would not occur. There was a paradox defining racial thought at the time. On the one hand, Confederates and their sympathizers argued that slaves were bloodthirsty insurrectionists, playing on fears of a situation similar to that in Haiti. On the other hand, it was argued that slaves were a docile people who followed their masters and always did their masters' bidding. But one cannot have it both ways. Once the insurrection did not occur, people could fall back on the position that blacks were docile. And this undercut Confederate propaganda.

QUESTION: You raised the question of importing cotton from India. Was there any sense of solidarity between the British working classes and Indians and the Sepoys?

ANSWER: Not that I know of. There was a bit of it in the wake of the Indian mutiny in 1857. But this was in the context of fears about people rising up and doing massive destruction to society. So for many British workers, the actions of those involved in the Indian mutiny were actually to be condemned rather than supported.

Let me add, along these lines, that around this time you see support for imperialism emerging within the British working classes. This escalated later on. But the elements were already in place during the American Civil War. I have noticed such feelings when working people debated about emigrating overseas. Many workers were saying that they should build up British colonies—particularly Australia—because they were part of the empire.

QUESTION: Your emphasis has been on public opinion in Great Britain about the Civil War. Can you tell us anything about public opinion in France at that time?

ANSWER: Historians have generally accepted the notion that the French were so solidly pro-Union at the time that there was nothing that the Confederates could do to influence French public opinion. So there has been very little study of French public opinion on the war.

What makes Britain so critical in all of this is its historical links with the United States, which included links between the working people and abolitionists in both countries. There were evangelical and philanthropic relationships that had been going on for thirty or forty years, based largely on antislavery activity. Blacks who had long been involved in that effort naturally put their emphasis on affecting international public opinion regarding the war by influencing the British to the Union side. I have, however, come across accounts of meetings in France after the assassination of Lincoln in which French people expressed themselves in ways similar to the British working class.

QUESTION: Where did those blacks who went to Great Britain come from? Were they runaway slaves or northern free blacks? Where did they acquire the ability to become public speakers?

ANSWER: The majority of them were fugitive slaves who had lived for a while in the North or in Canada. Many of them were self-taught, even while in slavery. They often felt their way through the art of public speaking. If you read accounts of their initial appearances, they were sometimes terrible. As they worked at it, they became increasingly proficient. And there had been, for twenty or thirty years, a long tradition of these people making public appearances in Britain. Many of them thus had quite a bit of speaking experience by the time the Civil War started.

QUESTION: But wouldn't white abolitionists have been concerned that fugitive slaves shouldn't be too proficient or articulate because they would lose their legitimacy as slaves? Wouldn't they be afraid that the British would not believe that the speakers were really former slaves if they spoke too well?

ANSWER: That was a question that was raised before the war, but by the time of the war, things had changed. By this time, the British were familiar enough with fugitive slaves that the ones who went to Britain no longer had to face the kinds of problems that Frederick Douglass faced when he first went over. Of course, you have to understand that it is very difficult to tell from the reporting of speeches in British newspapers just how proficient and articulate blacks were in the use of "proper English." When people wanted to criticize the fugitive slaves, they framed reports of their remarks in a garbled, racist, broken English. Remember that minstrelsy was very popular in England well into the twentieth century. The English were certainly capable of distorting black speech patterns.

QUESTION: Have you detected any links between independent black communities in England and the movement to support the Union and the northern abolition cause?

ANSWER: No. By this period, there was no black community left in London. The city's black community had all but disappeared through intermarriage and migration to West Africa and British colonies in the West Indies. I have seen allusions to a small group of fugitive slaves staying temporarily in London awaiting assistance to go on to West Africa—particularly to Liberia and Sierra Leone. There were two small black communities in Britain—one in Liverpool, the other developing in southern Wales near Cardiff. But these communities were not large enough to play any role in the recognition question.

NOTES

Research for this essay was made possible by a fellowship from the American Council of Learned Societies and support from the Research and University Graduate School, Indiana University.

1. Samuel Fielden, "Autobiography of Samuel Fielden," in Philip S. Foner, ed., *The Autobiographies of the Haymarket Martyrs* (New York, 1969), 142–43.

2. R. J. M. Blackett, *Building an Antislavery Wall: Black Americans in the Atlantic Abolitionist Movement, 1830–1860* (Baton Rouge, 1983), 20.

3. Donaldson Jordan and Edwin J. Pratt, *Europe and the American Civil War* (Boston, 1931), 178.

4. *Liverpool Mercury,* 26 June 1862; *Sunderland Times,* 11 May 1861.

5. *Midland Counties Herald,* 19 Dec. 1861.

6. Quoted in Jordan and Pratt, *Europe and the American Civil War,* 128.

7. *Bradford Review,* 19 Nov. 1863; *Index,* 19 Nov. 1863.

8. Henry Pilling, *America and the British Left: From Bright to Bevan* (New York, 1957), 3, 13.

9. "The Diary of John Ward of Clitheroe, Weaver, 1860–1864," *Transactions of the Historic Society of Lancashire and Cheshire* 105 (1953): 137–85; *Ashton and Stalybridge Reporter,* 9, 18 July 1863.

10. W. O. Henderson, *The Lancashire Cotton Famine, 1861–1865* (Manchester, 1934), 1; Neville Kirk, *The Growth of Working-Class Reform in Mid-Victorian England* (Urbana, 1985), 33; Frank L. Owsley, *King Cotton Diplomacy: Foreign Relations of the Confederate States of America,* 2d ed. (Chicago, 1959), 7–8.

11. Lord to Seward, Manchester, 13 Sept. 1861, Despatches from U.S. Consuls in Manchester, 1847–1906, National Archives, Washington, D.C.

12. *Bee Hive,* 2 Jan. 1864; Melvin Small, "Historians Look at Public Opinion," in Melvin Small, ed., *Public Opinion and Historians* (Detroit, 1970), 14–15; Jordan and Pratt, *Europe and the American Civil War,* 146.

13. Owsley, *King Cotton Diplomacy,* 442–43.

14. *Preston Chronicle,* 27 June 1863; *Oldham Standard,* 25 April 1863.

15. *Preston Chronicle,* 11 June 1863, 4 July 1863; *Preston Herald,* 9 May 1863, 20, 27 June 1863; *Preston Guardian,* 4 July 1863.

16. *Bristol Daily Post,* 2 Dec. 1864; *Ashton and Stalybridge Reporter,* 16 Aug. 1862, 31 Jan. 1863, 18 July 1863.

17. Howard Temperley, *British Antislavery, 1833–1870* (Columbia, S.C., 1972), 256; *Liberator,* 28 Feb. 1862; Betty Fladeland, *Men and Brothers: Anglo-American Anti-Slavery Cooperation* (Urbana, 1972), 396.

18. "Rules and Bye Laws of the Southern Club of Liverpool Established 1862," in Dudley Collection, Huntington Library; Spence to Mason, Liverpool, 15 Sept. 1862, in Mason Papers, Library of Congress; Charles Francis Adams to Seward, London, 18 Dec. 1862, Despatches from U.S. Ministers to Great Britain, 1791–1906, National Archives, Washington, D.C.; Morse to Seward, London, 8 Jan. 1863, Despatches of U.S. Consuls in London, England, 1790–1906, National Archives, Washington, D.C.; *Morning Star,* 4, 11 Dec. 1862.

19. *Index,* 31 Dec. 1862, 10, 17 March 1864; Hotze to Benjamin, London, 6 June 1863, in Hotze Papers, Library of Congress; Charles C. Cullop, *Confederate Propaganda in Europe 1861–1865* (Coral Gables, Fla., 1969), 94–95; Francis Tremlett to Mason, London, 2 June 1864, in Mason Papers.

20. *Todmorden Times,* 6 June 1863; *Morning Star,* 20 Oct. 1863, 12, 25 Dec. 1863.

21. Lord to Seward, Manchester, 20, 24 Sept. 1864, Despatches from U.S. Consuls in Manchester.

22. *Manchester Guardian,* 30 Jan. 1864; *Morning Star,* 29 Jan. 1863, 14 Feb. 1863.

23. *Ashton and Stalybridge Reporter,* 3 May 1862; Kirk, *The Growth of Working-Class Reform,* 64, 116; P. M. Peers, "The Cotton Famine in Ashton-under-Lyne, 1861–1865" (Manchester College of Education, 1970), 20, 30, 36. Almost one quarter of the thirty thousand employed in Glasgow's seventy mills were idle in November 1862. Many of those who were still at work were working only two to four days per week. Few were fully employed. *Glasgow Sentinel,* 6 Dec. 1862.

24. *Bee Hive,* 4 Oct. 1862; see also Edwin Waugh, *Home-Life of the Lancashire Factory Folk during the Cotton Famine* (London, 1867), 24.

25. Chartism was a radical working-class movement that gained its name from the six-point charter published in 1838 calling for fundamental reforms in British economic, social, and political life. The movement survived into the 1850s.

26. *Ashton and Stalybridge Reporter,* 7 Dec. 1861, 3 May 1862.

27. *Ashton and Stalybridge Reporter,* 3 May 1862, 9 June 1862, 16 Aug. 1862.

28. Virginia Mason, *The Public Life and Diplomatic Correspondence of James M. Mason* (Roanoke, Va., 1903), 293; Hotze to secretary of state, London, 25 April 1862, in Hotze Papers; Spence to Mason, Liverpool, 28 April 1862, in Mason Papers.

29. *Preston Guardian,* 2 July 1862; *Blackburn Standard,* 13 Aug. 1862.

30. *Manchester Examiner and Times,* 22, 26, 29 July 1862; *Bolton Guardian,* 26 July 1862.

31. Hotze to Benjamin, London, 26 Sept. 1862, in Hotze Papers.

32. Brian Jenkins, *Britain and the War for the Union,* 2 vols. (Montreal, 1980), 2:90.

33. Spence to Mason, Liverpool, 7 Dec. 1863, in Mason Papers; *Morning Star,* 1 Dec. 1863; *North British Daily Mail,* 12, 15 Dec. 1863.

34. *Bury Times,* 17 Oct. 1863; *Ashton and Stalybridge Reporter,* 6 Sept. 1862, 2 April 1864, 14 Jan. 1865.

35. *Ashton and Stalybridge Reporter,* 21, 28 Feb. 1863, 9, 23 May 1863; Betty Fladeland, *Abolitionists and Working-Class Problems in the Age of Industrialization* (Baton Rouge, 1984), 132; on Barker's successes elsewhere, see Mary Ellison, *Support for Secession: Lancashire and the American Civil War* (Chicago, 1972).

36. *Ashton and Stalybridge Reporter,* 25 June 1864.

37. Jenkins, *Britain & War for Union,* 2:31; *Bury Times,* 6 Feb. 1864, 2 July 1864; *Manchester Examiner and Times,* 14 Nov. 1863, 19 July 1864; *Salford News,* 16 July 23, 1864; *Index,* 31 Dec. 1863.

38. *Index,* 21 July 1864; *Manchester Examiner and Times,* 19 July 1864; *Reports of the Select Committee of the House of Commons on Public Petitions, Session 1863* (London, 1863), 243, 273, 342, 379–80; *Reports of the Select Committee of the House of Commons on Public Petitions, Session 1864* (London, 1864), 596, 629, 679, 750, 759, 843–46.

39. *Oldham Standard,* 29 April 1865.

40. Spence to Mason, Liverpool, 31 May 1864, in Mason Papers; Morse to Seward, London, 3 Feb. 1865, Despatches from U.S. Consuls in London; Jordon and Pratt, *Europe and the American Civil War,* 20.

41. Henderson, *The Lancashire Cotton Famine,* 8–9; Owsley, *King Cotton Diplomacy,* 545.

42. R. M. Paterson, "Newmilns' Weavers and the American Civil War," *Ayrshire Archeological and Natural History Collection,* 2d ser., 1 (1949): 98; *Ayr Advertiser,* Dec. 22, 1864.

NAPOLEON IS COMING!
MAXIMILIAN IS COMING?

The International History of the Civil War in the Caribbean Basin

★ ★ ★

THOMAS SCHOONOVER

As the inhabitants of Veracruz, Mexico, awoke on 8 December 1861, twenty-six Spanish vessels lay off the coast. This expeditionary force quickly overcame the local opposition and landed 6,000 Spanish troops. Mexican officials no longer governed their nation's major port. Within a few weeks, British and French naval vessels unloaded 700 British troops, 2,000 French soldiers, and 500 exotically colorful French Zouaves. Two queens, Spain's Isabella and Great Britain's Victoria, and an emperor, France's Napoleon III, seemed determined to decide the destiny of Mexico, even though they insisted that they only intended to collect overdue loans and protect their subjects.

France, Spain, and Britain had signed the Tripartite Treaty in November 1861 to lay the groundwork for the invasion. The decision triggered a five-year war between the French (with moral support from the Confederate government) and Mexican liberals (with some help from the United States). This drama's cast came to feature some of the leading figures of the age, including Abraham Lincoln, Jefferson Davis, William H. Seward,

Thaddeus Stevens, Ulysses S. Grant, William T. Sherman, Philip H. Sheridan, Benito Juárez, Porfirio Díaz, Napoleon III, Archduke Maximilian of Hapsburg, Princess Carlotta of Belgium, queens Isabella of Spain and Victoria of England, and field marshals Elie Forey and François Achille Bazaine. The intervention inspired scores of later films, novels, and popular histories and biographies. One of Mexico's principal national celebrations remains the Cinco de Mayo—in remembrance of 5 May 1862, when the Mexican army defeated the French at Puebla in a bloody day-long battle.

Why did these European powers feel compelled to intervene? What did they really expect from this military expedition? Were the European states capitalizing on the Civil War raging in the United States as a cover for their imperial expansion? Could the Union government, given the uncertainty of the war and its demand for men, material, and naval resources, afford to interpose against the European intrusions?

The arrival of Napoleon III, and later Maximilian, in Mexico were merely episodes in a long story whose chronology encompasses more than the Civil War years of 1861–65, whose geography extends far beyond Mexico, and whose geopolitics involves other European nations and other interventions in the New World. The remarks that follow intend to place the Civil War within its nineteenth-century international context.

Since the days of the buccaneers, North Americans had participated in a multinational competition to dominate the Gulf-Caribbean. We need to explore the importance of the Caribbean and Central American region to the Civil War protagonists. Or, to put it another way, we need to discover an international history of the Civil War in the Caribbean—the islands plus the mainland from Mexico down to Colombia and Venezuela. The terms circum-Caribbean and Gulf-Caribbean are convenient alternative designations for this region. In the nineteenth century, any nation aspiring to some measure of international power sought assured access to the isthmian transit and trade in the circum-Caribbean. So the Union and Confederate reaction to the European intervention in Mexico was one chapter in a story that spun out over several decades.

The Gulf-Caribbean Area: The Playing Field for U.S. and European Entrepreneurs, Expansionists, and Geopoliticians.

We can better comprehend the meaning of these events if we incorporate theory and historiography   what historians have written over the years—with some narrative. World-systems theory describes the relationship of classes and groups from metropole (core), semiperiphery, and periphery states within the world economy. This theory sees the world becoming a single economy. Metropoles not only control the factors of production—land, labor, and capital—and distribution, but also acquire the political power and technology to control factors of production and distribution in the periphery and semiperiphery. A semiperipheral state controls some of the factors of production, but not all. It functions both as exploiter and exploited in the world economy. A periphery region controls at most one of the factors of production. Metropole expansion commonly incorporates the periphery or semiperiphery into the world economy.[1]

Social imperialism defines a situation in which the preservation of well-being and security in the metropole rests on its ability to ameliorate domestic social woes through its ties to the periphery. Metropole states export the problems, the burdens, and the injustices of their political economy to peripheral areas. For example, in the mid-nineteenth century, many northerners favored the colonization of blacks in Africa or in the Gulf-Caribbean because their racism rejected the presence of blacks in U.S. society. In this case, foreign relations were being used to resolve a domestic social dilemma. When social problems drive expansionist conduct, we have social imperialism. Historically, social imperialism often established the dependent status of a peripheral society because the powerful metropole defined its well-being and tranquility in terms of access to the periphery. I use social imperialism to shed light on the impulses operating within the metropole states and dependency theory to illuminate the consequences of metropole intrusions into the periphery.[2]

Unfortunately, many U.S. historians of the middle period of the nineteenth century view events too parochially and do not take advantage of the insights that can be gleaned from world-systems theory. They have concerned themselves too narrowly with sectionalism, the primacy of cotton, southern exceptionalism, and failed southern nationalism. Studies of the Civil War dwell on military events, internal political and economic problems in the Union and Confederacy, and the war's personalities rather than the broader considerations of the war's meaning for mid-nineteenth-century international relations. The Civil War was not an entirely domestic affair.[3]

Historians of the Confederacy, for instance, focus too narrowly on the new nation's poor leadership, inadequate access to industrial products, and inability to awaken the nationalist impulses of the southern people so that they would bear the war's sacrifices. To break the poverty of this interpretation, historians need to consider that southerners also were at a disadvantage because of their flawed understanding of the links of southern society to the world system. The South lacked control over the factors of production, and thus existed as a peripheral area. Antebellum cotton producers acknowledged that web of relationships when they presumed that increased consumption of cotton textiles in Asia meant a rising price for their raw cotton. They considered this web in the narrowest manner, however. They seldom inquired about the source of investment to expand cotton textile production, to increase the distribution process, and to market the textiles, or about who would plan and manage the complicated processes of this market expansion. They rejoiced at the opportunity to sell more cotton to European merchants. Yet they were merely one step up the economic ladder from the slaves in a complex process involving the production, shipping, finance, manufacturing, and distribution of the raw material. The profits were distributed disproportionately higher up the ladder, closer to where major decisions managing the economic order were made. Astute southerners should have realized that peripheral areas—banana or coffee republics, for example—seldom profited much from major economic changes.[4]

In order to achieve a better comprehension of the Civil War, we might begin by observing that North Americans and Europeans had clashed repeatedly in the Caribbean area throughout the U.S. colonial period and in the early decades of independence. Those powers with Caribbean possessions—Britain, France, Spain, and the Netherlands—wished to secure (or to expand) their holdings. Spain guarded its island colonies jealously once its mainland colonies won independence in the early nineteenth century. Many Spanish leaders dreamed that these islands might form a base from which the mother country might reconquer imperial glory. Meanwhile Mexico, New Granada, several European states, and the United States lusted after Cuba and Puerto Rico. Their mutual jealousy, however, helped Spain to retain its islands.

The metropole powers looked beyond the Spanish islands as they sought advantage in the Caribbean. A few examples of European activity in the region illustrate the level of increasing involvement. The Dutch obtained the first concession for a canal across Central America in 1830. Belgians operated a large colonization concession near Santo Tomás in Guatemala in the late 1830s and 1840s. The British established a protectorate over the Mosquito Kingdom on the coast of Nicaragua and created a colony in the Bay Islands off Honduras. Carl, Prince of Prussia and brother to King William I, became involved in a colonization project in Nicaragua in the 1840s. France intrigued in Haiti and Santo Domingo and conducted the "Pastry War" in Mexico in 1838 to protect French subjects, property, and honor. Spanish officials offered aid to defeated Mexican conservatives in the 1840s and 1850s and plotted to restore friendly factions in Santo Domingo, Venezuela, and Colombia. Numerous other concessions and schemes involving colonization, land, communications, money, and arms peppered the Latin American landscape. Collectively, Europeans dominated the circum-Caribbean and were the principal investors. During this period, Britain tried to expand its strong position in the region. Spain and France sought to revive past grandeur through greater influence in the same area. Germany and Italy, states moving toward unification, expected to attain wealth and prestige through empire.[5]

Napoleon III had envisioned a revived French empire even before he achieved power. In the New World, he invoked shared "Latin" values to block Anglo-Saxon expansion. In the 1850s, French propagandist and promoter Félix Belly charged that Nicaragua was displeased with U.S. aid to filibustering and ready to grant favorable transit and colonization concessions if Europe could assure its independence. Napoleon III and Belly believed that the weaker Latin American states looked to Europe, especially France, to aid the "Latin" race to resist the Anglo-Americans.[6]

After the Napoleonic wars, the numerous German states moved slowly toward unification, and the leaders in some states—for example, Prussia and the Hansa cities—applied social imperialist strategies to Latin America. Beginning in the 1820s, Hansa, Rhine, and Ruhr entrepreneurs sought to use the local economies of the Caribbean region as a sponge for small but growing surpluses in textiles, iron wares, capital, and population, and as a supplier of additional raw materials and new products to improve German life-styles. Elements of the traditional aristocratic, military, and bureaucratic classes came to realize that foreign commercial and capital expansion could help combat the problems of an industrializing economy.[7] They hoped that if some unemployed people could be sent abroad, and if cheap raw materials were secured abroad, this would lower the cost of living at home and thus undermine socialist protest. Prussian privy councilor Franz Hugo Hesse advised his king that "German business activity and production are in the midst of irresistible growth, yet if this growth is to become a blessing and not a curse, Germany needs markets which could still be found in the Middle American states." Any policy that reduced unemployment, resisted the declining standard of living, and weakened social agitation and protest should have a dampening effect upon crime. One pitfall, however, was that many German migrants adopted other citizenship and were lost to the fatherland. Hesse's projects in the Caribbean area were designed to preserve the allegiance of the migrants, build a powerful position near a future interoceanic canal, and supply markets for manufactures. He wanted "Prussia to turn full attention to the states of Middle America in the interest of German trade and . . . to protect German emigration and colonization."[8] In the 1850s, about two thousand Germans migrated to Central America. In the 1860s, more arrived. They built clubs and schools, engaged successfully in agricultural, commercial, and financial affairs, and permanently established German interests and culture in Central America.[9]

The European powers recognized the value of the waist of the New World, which connected two half-globes, the Atlantic and the Pacific basin. The Suez Canal, completed in the 1850s, was an option that offered Europeans access to the east coast of Africa, the Red Sea area, south and southeast Asia, and the Australia–New Zealand region. But it was not particularly advantageous for trading with east Asia, the west coast of the New World, and the Pacific islands. Increasingly, Europeans saw the New World as a part of a world economic order.

Not all European "Latin" states had good relations with their cultural relatives in the New World. Spain's relations with Mexico were strained, largely because Spanish royalists could not resist meddling in Mexican affairs. In the 1850s, Mexican conservatives persuaded Spanish royalists that Mexicans would welcome a return to stronger civil and religious authority, possibly under a member of the royal house. Spanish royalists, religious leaders, and conservatives, unwilling to accept liberal rule as final, preferred to keep alive the vision of a restoration of its royal house in Mexico.[10]

Meanwhile, North Americans eyed the areas south with dreams of expansion, distrusted foreign presence in the region, and stood in the way of European projects. Even before the pronouncement of the Monroe Doctrine, U.S. geopoliticians, businessmen, and military leaders considered Latin America their special preserve. Monroe's famous doctrine reinforced the idea that this nation had a special mission in the New World. Though European leaders privately rejected the Monroe Doctrine, they normally tried to avoid direct confrontation with the United States in the pre–Civil War period.[11]

Nineteenth-century leaders in the United States, reflecting traditional concerns of Protestants about papal plots, worried about Catholic power lying across the entrance to the ports on the Gulf of Mexico from Florida to Texas. These ports were the outlet for the production of the Midwest as well as the South. Ever-increasing exports of processed foodstuffs, timber products, and semi- and fully manufactured products that the American domestic market could not absorb underscored this nation's vital interests in the Caribbean basin.[12]

U.S. officials reacted to European challenges in the circum-Caribbean during the 1840s and 1850s with a variety of responses. They negotiated the Bidlack Treaty (1846) to assure U.S. transit at Panama; the Clayton-Bulwer Treaty (1850), which neutralized competition for a Central American canal; and the Gadsden purchase of territory from Mexico, which was deemed essential if a southern transcontinental railroad was to be constructed to the Pacific coast. American representatives abroad authored the Ostend Manifesto, an attempt to acquire Cuba.[13] Both northerners and southerners supported some, but not all, of the diplomatic initiatives.

The tension between North and South was not confined to domestic affairs but was reflected in international relations and conflicting worldviews. The commercial agrarianism of the South differed from the commercial industrialization of the North in matters of investment, communications, and financial policy, although both societies expected expansion to foster well-being and security. Leaders north of the Mason-Dixon line were more captivated by the European liberal thought and institutions that permeated the world economy. Southern leaders were trying to preserve an anachronistic social and labor system and to achieve ill-considered world objectives that would perpetuate the region's dependence on foreign capital, distribution, and even labor.[14]

Both northerners and southerners considered the New World as fit for their expansionist inclinations. At times, however, they differed about where to expand and for what purpose. The highly respected scientist and future Confederate naval officer Matthew Fontaine Maury prescribed a course of empire that southern leaders should have heeded. He envisioned transit to the Pacific as vital: "I regard the Pacific railroad and a commercial thoroughfare across the Isthmus as links in the same chain, parts of the great whole which . . . is to effect a revolution in the course of trade. . . . Those two works . . . are not only necessary fully to develop the immense resources of the Mississippi valley . . . but . . . their completion would place the United States on the summit level of commerce." The isthmus region was, in his view, the "barrier that separates us from the markets of six hundred millions of people—three fourths of the population of the earth. Break it down . . . and this country is placed midway between Europe and Asia; this [Gulf of Mexico and the Caribbean] becomes the centre of the world and the focus of the world's commerce."[15] Few southern, or later Confederate, leaders acted upon Maury's geopolitics. Many were more interested in territorial land-grabs than in enhancing the region's commercial outlets.

Adventurers from the United States plunged into about a dozen filibustering expeditions before the Civil War. Southern leaders guided those that invaded Latin American nations and dependencies of European powers, intending to expand the slave-labor and plantation systems. Robert May has written about many of the filibusters, such as John Quitman, William Walker, and Henry L. Kinney, as well as their commercial boosters, such as Jane and William Cazneau and Joseph Fabens, as they pursued "Southern dreams of a Caribbean empire." An earlier Purdue historian, Louis Martin Sears, wrote a fine biography of Louisianan John Slidell—a friend of southern filibustering. Meanwhile, northern entrepreneurs, merchants, and shippers were active in the Panama Railroad; Cornelius Vanderbilt's Accessory Transit Company in Nicaragua; the Tehuantepec railroad companies, which sought to establish a transit route across Mexico's narrow neck; E. George Squier's Honduran Interoceanic Railroad, and a host of steamship companies tying U.S. east coast ports to the Caribbean and isthmus. They supported filibusters who might facilitate access to the Pacific basin. Thomas Hietala, noting the social imperialist intent behind much of antebellum U.S. expansionism, renamed it "manifest design" instead of "manifest destiny."[16]

Spanish and Costa Rican leaders were aware that the very success of northern liberals in imprinting a free-soil policy on territories in the western areas of the United States probably meant increased southern filibustering pressure upon their empires or nations. Costa Rican officials pondered their nation's fate as the North prevented slavery from expanding into Kansas: "Where might the South direct its vision in order to fulfill its goals, to repair its losses, and to perpetuate its expensive institution? . . . The South will look towards Mexico, Cuba, and Central America. The absorption of these countries is a fact, offered and decreed by those in power, announced by many people, and consented to by all opponents."[17] Gabriel García y Tassara, Spanish minister in the United States, shared their expectations: "It seems evident that the proslavery faction is going to consider a policy of annexation and filibustering to obtain compensation for the major and inevitable reverse which its principle [the right to extend slavery into the national territories] is going to experience [in Kansas]. . . . What is important for us to know or to calculate is the range which these potshots might come to have. Cuba is always the grand perspective, but not more than a perspective."[18] These Hispanic leaders ascribed a social imperialist response to frustrated southerners who would seek to ameliorate their deteriorating domestic situation with foreign expansion.

One must understand this foreign activity and the North American response to it to comprehend the Civil War era within its international context. We cannot divorce secession, Civil War, and Reconstruction from the long-standing international conflict between liberalism and conservatism, which flourished in the New World as well as Europe. Liberalism, expressed in the works of Adam Smith and John Stuart Mill, emphasized the need for liberty in an open, accessible economic, social, and political order. This meant a free-market economic system but also the end of slavery, which was forced labor, not free labor. Liberalism proclaimed that well-being, self-reliance, and progress came out of the marketplace. Liberals also wanted to reduce the role of government. Generally they accepted urban, secular, and materialistic life-styles. Conservatives, on the other hand, were aristocratic, religiously oriented, patriarchal, and suspicious of common people. They valued rural life and rejected the commercial and industrial goals of the liberals.[19]

Both North and South struggled for greater control of their own destinies, the South as a peripheral state, the North as a semiperipheral one. The South depended upon Europe for capital and a distribution network. It also relied upon imported labor—slaves. Northern liberals even made the access of southerners to sufficient land for their system's continuation uncertain. By the mid-nineteenth century, the North had achieved semiperipheral status because it possessed ample land and a sophisticated distribution system rooted in its large, experienced merchant and shipping enterprises; yet it lacked technology (a form of capital), commonly needed more and cheaper labor, and could not finance its growth. So Britain and other European metropoles exploited the northern states, which in turn exploited the South, extracting wealth through business activity and the capacity to use political processes. Northerners were able to obtain access to labor (by facilitating European immigration), inland transportation, and federal revenue policy. Commerce on the upper Mississippi and Ohio rivers was well served by the Army Corps of Engineers. Meanwhile, northerners denied southerners access to both the African slave trade and much of the public domain. Peripheral areas such as the South rely upon simple economic structures bound to the world economy by the slender threads of a few basic products. Alternative sources of the products or altered consumption patterns can quickly undermine the impact of peripheral states upon the world economy. In this sense, cotton served the same role that bananas would play for Central American countries decades later.[20]

For the North to achieve metropole status, it had to take advantage of domestic accumulation and exploit areas of the periphery (including the South) or semiperiphery. Given the hold of the metropoles on the processes of accumulation and their advantages in technology, such a transformation would be difficult, but not impossible.[21] The Caribbean region offered an obvious location where North American businessmen might try to control the material value produced by other people.

Now that we understand the international rivalry already in progress in the circum-Caribbean before Fort Sumter, we can turn to what happened during the Civil War. Most historians have neglected the story of Confederate interest in the Caribbean. American scholars writing on international relations during the Civil War have focused on Confederate efforts to gain diplomatic recognition, to break the Union blockade and trade cotton for European manufactures, and to attract foreign loans. Almost everything has been European oriented. Even Confederate activity in the Caribbean is interpreted in regard to the region's role as intermediary in trade with Europe. Scholars need to give a more satisfactory assessment of the role of the Caribbean in the Civil War. The Confederacy appointed about half of its foreign agents to posts in the Caribbean–Central American area. What was going on?

Confederate leaders viewed the circum-Caribbean as useful for trading cotton for European manufactures, buccaneering, and territorial expansion. But the war nudged expansionism off center stage temporarily. The West Indian islands and Mexico served as way stations for blockade runners and as rest stops for Confederate citizens traveling to or from Europe. But the circum-Caribbean offered far more enticing objectives for the Confederacy. The isthmus was home to two transcontinental transit routes, the Panama Railroad and the waterways of Nicaragua, which conveyed gold from California to the east. For many in the Confederate elite, the presence of Union treasure ships in the area offered the kind of lure that once had attracted Drake and the buccaneers to the region.[22]

The circum-Caribbean was an ideal place for planning, organizing, and outfitting ventures to seize Union gold. Havana provided a chief spot for planning and organizing; Panama and Colón were secondary places. Mexico, Belize, Honduras, and the Bay Islands served as staging areas for raiding parties that moved across the isthmus to use several Pacific ports to board gold-carrying vessels in small numbers so they would be less likely to be noticed. These raiding parties did not capture any gold vessels, but northern forces captured some members of the raiding parties.[23] Perhaps Dixie's leadership, caught up in romantic memories of past buccaneers, put too much faith in these raiding parties. The Confederate government would have been better off concentrating on commercial initiatives.

But excessive confidence in the power of "king cotton" was so endemic in the Confederacy that it crippled the new nation's ability to make the most out of commercial opportunities available to it. Cotton barons, deeply in debt to British merchants and financiers, holding a raw material that was not scarce, and operating in a complex production and distribution system, failed to weigh impartially their economic and political power. Cotton was not king, and it never had been. It was neither a prince nor a knight. It was closer to Falstaff, a figure near power who was sometimes perceptive, often not, and at times comic or pretentious. Cotton bound the South to European metropoles.[24]

Without understanding the ways in which their political economy was structurally integrated into the world system, the Confederate leadership stumbled toward policies intended to effect a separation from the northern states and to allow the South to develop its version of economic growth. The Civil War freed them from unfriendly northern leaders who opposed any expansion of forced labor, which was inconsistent with a liberal, free market economic order.[25] But as long as the South relied upon a discontented and potentially rebellious labor force, exhausted land, and borrowed capital to produce a single export-crop that was not a scarce material, it would remain on the periphery of the world system.[26] If the leaders of the Confederacy were to obtain a stronger voice in the future of their society, they needed greater control over the domestic factors of production and distribution and ultimately, most likely, over the factors of production in nearby areas.

King cotton assumptions rested upon the belief that Europe needed southern cotton, whereas all it really needed was fibers for textile production. Therefore, when the Civil War in the United States reduced exports of southern cotton across the Atlantic, European textile mills and consumers around the world located alternative sources of cotton, switched to alternative fibers, or developed alternative consumption patterns to mitigate the cotton shortage. Dissatisfied with political dependency on the North, the South rebelled to become an independent state in the mistaken view that independent political authority would alter its economic relationship to the world. Its economic dependence upon Great Britain (and Europe) hampered its self-sufficiency and self-governing as much as its political dependence on the North. To accumulate wealth and transform their economy into a semiperipheral one, and thus achieve real independence, southerners needed to participate in the production, finance, and distribution facilities of the world economy.[27]

Some Confederates did recognize the tactical importance of the isthmus for waging commercial war on the Union, and some even saw improved transit as a means for expanding the distribution of raw cotton (to Asia) and finding an outlet for a new raw material, the ores of the Southwest. A few southerners even perceived the significance of transcontinental communications for the future of an independent state. Some recognized the possibility of using the Middle American mainland for trading and even recruiting. In ports such as Matamoros, Tampico, and Belize, Confederate agents traded cotton for European products and moved small numbers of recruits to the South.

Karl Marx's comment on humanity's ability to influence history perhaps describes the dilemma of the Confederate officials: "Men make their own history, but they don't make it just as they please; they do not make it under circumstances chosen by themselves, but under circumstances directly encountered, given, and transmitted from the past."[28] Cotton planters and southern politicians accepted dependence and peripheral status without making sustained efforts before or during the Civil War to alter such patterns. These elites were often coopted. They shared to some modest degree in the wealth being generated, and acquiesced in the continuation of a subordinate role for their society in the world economy. The Confederate leaders bore the burden of continuity with their traditions because most had ignored the vision and geopolitics of men such as Maury or had failed to create their own realistic vision of their world.

The Union's leaders, especially Seward, did recognize the need to fit the United States into a world economy. Seward had outlined such objectives since the 1840s and 1850s. He spoke out strongly for territorial and commercial expansion. He expected the United States to serve as an intermediary between the civilizations of the East and West, which would "mingle . . . on our own free soil, and a new and more perfect civilization will arise to bless the earth, under the sway of our own cherished and beneficent democratic institutions."[29] Seward believed that annexation might be the proper long-range course for U.S. relations with Latin America. In 1860 he claimed that "amid all the convulsions that are breaking the Spanish American republics, and in their rapid decay and dissolution, [he saw] the preparatory stage for their reorganization in free, equal and self-governing members of the United States."[30]

Yet even in the 1850s, when U.S. presidents seemed bent on acquiring new possessions, Seward placed commercial expansion above territorial expansion. He wanted the United States "to command the empire of the seas, which alone is real empire," and this would advance the U.S. position in the "commerce of the world, which is the empire of the world." In the Senate, he explained the ties of industry to commerce and empire: "Put your domain under cultivation and your ten thousand wheels of manufacture in motion. The nation that draws most materials and provisions from the earth, and fabricates the most, and sells the most of production and fabrics to foreign nations, must be, and will be, the great power of the earth."[31] Seward and other liberal expansionists proposed rail, steam, and telegraph communications to link the U.S. economy with Latin America, the Pacific islands, and east, southeast, and south Asia. Seward's territorial expansionism served a secondary purpose to his overriding commercial goals.

During the Civil War, U.S. minister to Mexico Thomas Corwin, Postmaster General Montgomery Blair, Seward, and others considered territorial acquisitions in regard to social imperialist schemes to colonize U.S. blacks in the Caribbean–Central American area. These colonies would not simply resolve the United States' racial dilemma; they would also bolster the U.S. presence and influence nearly all potential interoceanic transit routes. Talks produced preliminary terms for black colonies in Mexico, British Honduras, Guatemala, Honduras, and Costa Rica before the U.S. government's insistence upon the colonists' retaining U.S. citizenship caused a collapse of negotiations. The Lincoln administration did authorize schemes to settle a few hundred blacks on the isthmus or in the

Caribbean, but no permanent U.S. colony emerged. After this rejection, Seward returned to the idea that investment, trade, and steamer services were more desirable goals than territorial expansion. He succinctly defined the new view: U.S. leaders had learned to "value dollars more and dominion less."[32] Alaska, for example, was acquired in 1867 to support trade with Japan, Korea, and north China, not for its value as new territory.

Many northern leaders hoped to create order and development at home through liberal, free-market economics. They had to stop the separation of land, labor, and capital from the national market that the Confederacy represented, and then preserve areas for future expansion—such as the Caribbean—from European encroachment. Liberalism's growth-or-decay duality interpreted secession as a threat to reduce the nation's well-being and progress and to undermine its independence and growth. Secession implied a difficult future for the North and West and an increased possibility of a decaying social order. Since 1607 North Americans had proclaimed expansion, not contraction, as their destiny. In 1860 Walt Whitman's poem "A Broadway Pageant" captured the commercial essence at the heart of the liberal empire:

> I chant the world on my Western seas,
> . . . .
> I chant the new empire grander than any before, as in a vision it
>   comes to me,
> I chant America, the mistress, I chant a greater supremacy,
> I chant projected a thousand blooming cities yet in time on
>   those groups of sea-islands,
> My sail-ships and steam-ships threading the archipelagoes,
> My stars and stripes fluttering in the wind,
> Commerce opening, the sleep of ages having done its work,
>   races, reborn, refresh'd, . . .

Victory in the Civil War could end the internal threat to slice off factors of production and market area.[33]

However, the Civil War fixed U.S. attention inward and weakened the nation's capacity to resist encroachments in nearby areas. France, Spain, Britain, Austria, and Belgium challenged the U.S. vision for the Caribbean during the war. European nations intruded in various places in addition to Mexico, testing the U.S. government's ability to sustain its prewar influence in the Caribbean basin.

The French adventure in Mexico represented the most blatant challenge to U.S. aspirations in the Gulf-Caribbean region during the Civil War because of its size, duration, and the illustrious royalty involved— Emperor Napoleon III, Archduke Maximilian of Hapsburg, and Princess Carlotta of Belgium. In 1862, Napoleon III outlined France's task in the New World to General Forey:

> The prosperity of America . . . nourishes our industry and gives life to our commerce. We are interested in seeing the United States powerful and prosperous, but we have no interest in seeing that republic acquire the whole of the Gulf of Mexico, dominate from this vantage-point the Antilles and South America, and become the sole dispenser of the products of the New World. Mistress of Mexico, and consequently, of Central America and of the passage between two seas, there would be henceforth no other power in America than the United States. . . . [But if successful in Mexico,] we shall have opposed an insuperable barrier to the encroachments of the United States, we shall have maintained the independence of our colonies in the Antilles . . . and this influence . . . will create immense markets for our commerce, and will procure the materials indispensable to our industry.[34]

Napoleon III also cited "Latin" ties to justify French military support of the conservatives in Mexico.

Under the Tripartite Treaty of November 1861, which I alluded to earlier, France, as well as Britain and Spain, agreed to send troops into Mexico in response to the failure of the Mexican government, then headed by liberal president Juárez, to pay its foreign debt. The idea, on paper, was to force Mexico to pay reparations. But Napoleon intended, all along, to place Ferdinand Maximilian, the Austrian archduke, on a Mexican throne.

Seward tried to ward off this intervention by authorizing Corwin to offer a loan to the Juárez government that would help it service the Mexican debt. These instructions led to the pathbreaking Corwin–Manuel María

Zamacona Treaty of 1861—the first direct loan ever negotiated by the United States with a foreign government. However, the U.S. Congress, struggling with the financial strain of the war against the Confederacy, refused that obligation.

So French open defiance of the Monroe Doctrine encountered only muted resistance at first from the United States. What hampered Napoleon III's adventure the most, in the short run, was unexpectedly stiff military resistance from Juárez's Mexican liberals. Juárez, who remains one of Mexico's most popular, heroic figures, found moral and material support throughout Latin America and the United States. In addition, Napoleon III could not hold his tripartite alliance together. Both Great Britain and Spain had ambitions in the Gulf-Caribbean area, but neither found French intentions regarding Maximilian in their national interest.[35]

Spanish leaders dreamed of reasserting their nation's monarchical authority in the New World. In fact, the Spanish had initially answered Napoleon III's call in the belief that the Mexicans wanted a Spanish prince to govern their war-torn society. Civil war had raged in Mexico during the years preceding the tripartite intervention. Once it became clear that Napoleon III and Mexican conservatives had no intention of accepting a Spanish pretender, Spain withdrew from Mexico and sought to revive its lost glory elsewhere. Just as opportunistic about the Civil War in the United States as the French, Spanish forces reestablished order in and occupied civil-war-torn Santo Domingo in 1862. In 1863, Spanish forces blockaded several ports in Peru and Chile and occupied one Peruvian island. Almost every Latin American state and the U.S. government protested Spain's role in Mexico, Santo Domingo, and Peru. Spain would pull out of Santo Domingo and Peru in 1865 and 1866, respectively.[36]

The British government withdrew from Napoleon III's enterprise in Mexico once it became obvious that the French intended to challenge U.S. security and political interests. A decade earlier, British leaders had made a policy decision that their country should concentrate, when it came to the Gulf-Caribbean area, on economic benefits and access to interoceanic transit. British leaders believed that good relations with the United States would best facilitate their plans and hoped to avoid challenging U.S. security objectives in the region whenever possible. It had no interest in helping to build a puppet regime for Napoleon III and thereby angering the United States. A few years later, British subjects pursued an interoceanic mail route over Costa Rica and a transcontinental railroad in Nicaragua. British money also revived the Honduran Interoceanic Railroad, which had suspended construction in 1860.[37]

Given U.S. objections to the intervention in Mexico, Napoleon III's government wished to avoid additional challenges, as became apparent when a French company that was making progress in negotiations for a canal in Nicaragua requested a French war vessel to carry the Legion of Honor for Nicaragua's president and decorations for seven other Nicaraguans. The French cabinet rejected the idea because the medals would lose value if so distributed, and a war vessel might provoke a new U.S. invasion, since the project would appear to be under French protection. Yet France did want to secure its toehold in the Gulf-Caribbean. It contacted Guatemala and Belgium about reorganizing Belgium's colony at Santo Tomás, one of the better harbors on the Gulf of Mexico, which the French hoped to make a powerful military point in the Gulf. France also pursued efforts to acquire either a canal or railroad concession from Nicaragua as a further step to assure its power in the Gulf and to open interoceanic transit under covert French supervision.[38]

All these initiatives by European powers, especially the Mexican intervention, seemed to threaten the economic and strategic interests of the United States. U.S. industry had limited prospects for competing well in the highly industrialized and technologically advanced European markets. Without the courage to use the domestic market to develop a just and humane society, U.S. leaders looked to Latin America and Asia as the most attractive areas of future growth to sustain their vision of progress and well-being. Since trade with Asia required cheap, quick communications across the isthmus, access to the whole Pacific basin depended upon U.S. power and influence in the circum-Caribbean. Thus European action in Latin America in the early 1860s threatened the U.S. future in Asia as well as in Latin America. Both the Republican and Democratic parties wished to prevent new and reduce old foreign inroads into an area that was considered part of the U.S. economic sphere.[39]

Though absorbed by the domestic difficulties of the Civil War, Union policymakers kept an eye on European thrusts in the Gulf-Caribbean and particularly questioned the motivation behind the European intervention in Mexico. In addition to undercutting U.S. influence in Latin America, the intervention aided the conservative Mexicans and the Confederates and weakened liberal and republican institutions everywhere in the New World. The anti-American goal of Napoleon III's intervention intensified the desire of many Americans not only to eliminate his puppet, Maximilian, from the Cactus Throne but also to reassert U.S. preeminence throughout the Caribbean region. North American opponents of the French intervention organized numerous Monroe Doctrine leagues and Mexican clubs that sent material aid to Mexico and helped arouse public opinion in favor of removing the French and Maximilian. But the Lincoln administration rejected any assertion of the Monroe Doctrine by name while the Civil War was in progress, insisting, however, that its principles would be maintained. U.S. government leaders, President Juárez, and many Latin American leaders agreed that the French intervention must be resisted, but they disagreed about the best means of challenging it. Under Seward's leadership, the United States refused to participate in a Pan-American movement, the counteraction that most Latin American states favored.[40]

Maximilian blamed the negative reaction to his government in the United States on a Juárez-sponsored press campaign. But Maximilian's well-funded counterpublicity proved unavailing, which suggests that sentiment was indeed overwhelmingly opposed to a foreign monarchy in Mexico. Napoleon III's interest in Mexico waned after the Union victory in the Civil War and Prussia's defeat of Denmark and Austria in the 1860s on its way to unification of Germany. France redirected its attention to Europe. In April 1867, the last French troops withdrew, and Maximilian's forces were quickly defeated. He was captured, tried, and executed. Both Napoleon III and Maximilian were gone![41]

It should be noted that during the Lincoln administration, significant aspects of the controversy between radical (antislavery) and moderate Republicans on one hand and conservative Republicans on the other were based upon different foreign as well as domestic policies. While Lincoln's administration pursued policies to persuade France to withdraw from Mexico without conflict, radical and moderate Republicans urged more confrontational policies against the French intervention. This divergence continued when Andrew Johnson assumed the presidency after Lincoln's death. It even played a role in his impeachment. A growing interventionist sentiment in the United States complicated the early postwar years by intertwining a major but controversial foreign-relations problem with the serious domestic disagreements.[42]

To summarize, Confederate leaders sought short-term benefits in Central America and the Caribbean during the Civil War. They wanted places to trade cotton for arms, medicine, and other necessities, profits from privateering, and the chance to disturb U.S. naval and commercial activity. They were willing to suspend their expansionist dreams in the search for victory. Northern leaders sought short-term benefits and wished to retain their long-term objectives, trade and transit; but the Civil War temporarily delayed their efforts to prevent European penetration of the Caribbean basin.

It should not surprise us that in the postwar years, a reunited nation rejected European attempts to stymie U.S. expansion and acquisition of transit rights in the area. United States policymakers had particular success regarding Mexico. The Liberal Party in Mexico and the Republican Party in the United States shared an ideology—laissez-faire liberalism—which led them to define their respective problems and the solutions to their problems as interrelated, thus permitting the mutually desired American economic penetration of Mexico in the 1860s and 1870s.

However, the defeat of Napoleon III's dream did not end Europe's expansionism. The British continued to trade, invest, and work to secure access to isthmian transit. The Spanish became even more active in commerce and investment in the late nineteenth century and ultimately turned to culture—the *hispanismo* movement, which sought to revive pride in shared language, history, and customs—as a strategy to preserve its ties to Latin America in the face of the challenge of Pan-Americanism. Italian economic and diplomatic activity increased, as did Italian migration to Central America.[43]

In the late 1860s, as Prussia unified Germany, its navy, diplomats, and merchants were searching for naval stations in Asia, the Pacific, and the New World. Chancellor Otto von Bismarck was attracted by an offer of Civil War general and speculator John C. Frémont to sell his "rights" to build a Costa Rican railroad and naval station to the Prussian government, but premature publicity undermined Bismarck's plans. In 1878 a half dozen German vessels gathered off Nicaragua's coasts, and a landing party seized Corinto temporarily. By the 1890s, Germans controlled well over half of Guatemala's principal export, coffee.[44] Germany's economic and political role on the isthmus continued to grow in the late nineteenth and early twentieth centuries.

Napoleon III's mistake imposed no permanent burden upon France, nor did it end French Gulf-Caribbean ventures. In the 1870s, French promoters led the way in organizing a canal project. Some favored a Nicaraguan route, but most followed the engineer of the Suez Canal, Ferdinand de Lesseps, to Panama. The Panama Canal project revived French commerce, migration, and investment on the isthmus and in the Caribbean. By the 1890s, France was the second-largest investor on the isthmus, threatening Britain's leading position.

This continued European activity teaches us to review any assumptions we might harbor that Napoleon III and Maximilian ventured into Mexico solely because the Civil War temporarily weakened the U.S. ability to resist properly. The U.S. government and its military and business leaders had to respond to European activity in the circum-Caribbean in the post–Civil War decades just as they had done in the early nineteenth century. Somebody has always been coming to the Caribbean region: the Spanish, British, monarchists, or papists before the Civil War; and the French, bolsheviks, fascists, or communists since then. Napoleon III and Maximilian were part of a historic crowd of real and imaginary interlopers.

QUESTION: Did the Germans go down as far south as Colombia?

ANSWER: Even further than that. Many Germans settled and invested throughout Latin America. They were quite numerous in Colombia, and there were large settlements of Germans in Brazil, Argentina, and Chile. They came to stay because they built schools immediately. The three best schools in Guatemala right now, in fact, are the Swiss school, the Austrian school, and the German school. We are talking here of the equivalents of our elementary, junior high, and high schools.

QUESTION: Why did the Germans put such emphasis on schools in Latin America?

ANSWER: One of the ways the Germans tried to transfer their culture and to influence the elites in the area was by building schools. The schools served two functions. Initially, the purpose was to preserve the German-ness of the settlers. I mentioned that the loss of Germanness was one of the things that bothered Franz Hugo Hesse and the German government. When Germans migrated to the United States, too many of them became American citizens. The German authorities did not like that. They needed to get rid of the surplus population, so they tolerated it, but it wasn't good. Hesse argued that by sending the surplus population to Mexico and Costa Rica and places like that, they would preserve their Germanness. He negotiated agreements with these governments that allowed the Germans to build schools and churches and maintain their Germanness. So they built schools right away—and clubs. The French were more likely to take over someone else's schools. They sent teachers to Middle America to teach French in the existing Costa Rican or Salvadoran or Mexican schools. But the Germans built their own schools.

A second function of the schools was to attract children of elite and upper-middle-class families. Some might even pursue higher education in Germany, which could further strengthen their attachment to German culture. Later these children would assume elevated positions in the political economies of their native lands.

QUESTION: Did the French ever consider that the South might win the Civil War?

ANSWER: For the French, it didn't make much difference who won. The winner would be Anglo-Saxon and not Latin. So regardless of who won, the French still needed what Napoleon III referred to as a barrier against Anglo-Saxon power gaining control of the Caribbean and the isthmus and thereby becoming the dominant power in the area and the dispenser of all New World products and maybe even of the Asian trade. It was all right, apparently, for a Latin power to become dominant.

QUESTION: Was Napoleon III aware of the impact that a split power in the United States might have on the balance of power in the New World?

ANSWER: Yes, but the geopolitics of distance also comes into play here. France would be weaker than either the Union or an independent Confederacy in the New World. It would not have the troops or naval strength to compete with either the North or the South, even if France secured a couple of naval stations in the area. Napoleon's trick, of course, was to try to persuade the Hispanic nations that they were not to focus on the narrow Hispanicism but rather the broader Latinism, which also allowed France a closer relationship. If they accepted a Latin definition of their culture, then those peoples would become allies of, or sympathetic to tutelage by, the French or the European Latin powers. Later in the century, when the Spanish fostered the *hispanismo* movement, they included the French and Italians in their vision. They were more inclusive than Napoleon III had been. Napoleon said Latin, but he meant French!

QUESTION: Did any of the Latin American countries ever consider interceding on behalf of the Union or the Confederacy?

ANSWER: Not that I am aware of. The closest thing that I can think of is that Juárez was very sympathetic to the Union, and he gave permission for Union troops to use Mexican soil if it would prove beneficial to move troops from Guaymas into Arizona. The Mexican Liberals were also willing to allow northern vessels to use their harbors, and they agreed to deny Confederate commerce raiders a similar privilege. This different treatment was not an act of war, but it was an act that was beneficial to one side and not to the other.

Maximilian, in contrast, leaned toward the Confederacy. His field commanders were willing to let Confederate troops move to the Mexican side of the border to escape attack late in the war. Some of his generals allowed Confederates refuge on Mexican soil. The French normally were also tolerant of Confederate agents or soldiers in transit on Mexican soil if they were on some mission or were in the act of returning to the Confederacy. They observed the presence of Confederates in Mexico, but did not try to arrest or detain them.

NOTES

1. On the world system, see Immanuel Wallerstein, *The Modern World-System,* 3 vols. (Orlando, 1974–88), esp. 3:127–256; Wallerstein, *Historical Capitalism* (New York, 1983); Wallerstein, "The Rise and Future Demise of the World Capitalist System: Concepts for Comparative Analysis," *Comparative Studies in Society and History* 16 (1974): 387–415; Fernand Braudel, *Civilization and Capitalism: The Fifteenth–Eighteenth Centuries,* 3 vols. (New York and Orlando, 1979–84), esp. 3:17–88; Terence K. Hopkins and Immanuel Wallerstein, eds., *World-Systems Analysis: Theory and Methodology* (Beverly Hills, 1982); Christopher Chase-Dunn, "Core-Periphery Relations: The Effects of Core Competition," in Barbara Hockey Kaplan, ed., *Social Change in the Capitalist World Economy* (Beverly Hills, 1978), 159–76.

2. Bernard Semmel, *Imperialism and Social Reform, 1885–1914* (Cambridge, England, 1967); Hans-Ulrich Wehler, *Der Aufstieg des amerikanischen Imperialismus* (Göttingen, 1974), 37–73; Fernando Cardoso and Enzo Faletto, *Dependency and Development in Latin America* (Berkeley, 1979); Thomas Schoonover, *The United States in Central America, 1860–1911: Episodes of Social Imperialism and Imperial Rivalry in the World System* (Durham, NC, 1991), introduction.

3. Richard E. Beringer et al., *Why the South Lost the Civil War* (Athens, Ga., 1986); Archer Jones, *Confederate Strategy from Shiloh to Vicksburg* (Baton Rouge, 1961), 16–32; and E. Merton Coulter, *The Confederate States of America* (Baton Rouge, 1950), 19, argue that the Confederacy had no grand strategy other than the defense of territory and ending the blockade. This is a fairly common perspective, often with minor variations. See also Charles W. Ramsdell, *Behind the Lines in the Southern Confederacy* (Baton Rouge, 1944), 83–122; and Robert C. Black, III, "Thoughts on the Confederacy," in Donald Sheehan

and Harold C. Syrett, eds., *Essays in American Historiography: Papers Presented in Honor of Allan Nevins* (New York, 1960), 20–36. The old argument that the Confederacy defended race relations is without merit. The blacks were brought to the New World as a labor force that allowed a landed gentry to gather extensive social and personal accumulation.

4. Schoonover, *The United States in Central America,* chap. 1 and appendix; Wallerstein, "The Rise and Future Demise"; Hopkins and Wallerstein, eds., *World-Systems Analysis.* The documentation for this essay was found in numerous archives in Europe, Central America, Mexico, and the United States. Rather than repeat a minuscule portion of the sources here, I shall refer to my publications where the documentation is cited fully. The reader of these notes should thus consider the frequent references to my work as shorthand citations to the relevant public and private manuscripts.

5. Walter LaFeber, *The American Age: United States Foreign Policy at Home and Abroad since 1750* (New York, 1989), 69–147; Lester Langley, *Struggle for the American Mediterranean: United States–European Rivalry in the Gulf-Caribbean, 1776–1904* (Athens, Ga., 1976), 25–106; Hendrik Dane, *Die wirtschaftlichen Beziehungen Deutschlands zu Mexiko und Mittelamerika im 19. Jahrhundert* (Cologne, 1971), 78–151; Thomas Schoonover, "Metropole Rivalry in Central America, 1820s to 1929: An Overview," in Ralph Lee Woodward, Jr., ed., *Central America: Historical Perspective on the Contemporary Crisis* (Westport, Conn., 1988), 21–46.

6. John Leddy Phelan, "Pan-Latinism, French Intervention in Mexico (1861–1867) and the Genesis of the Idea of Latin America," in *Conciencia y autenticidad históricas* (Mexico, 1968), 279–98; Cyril Allen, *France in Central America: Felix Belly and the Nicaraguan Canal* (New York, 1966); Thomas Schoonover, "France in Central America, 1820s to 1930: An Overview," *Revue française d'histoire d'outre mer* 79 (1992): 161–97.

7. Thomas Schoonover, "German Penetration of Central America, 1820s–1930," *Jahrbuch für Geschichte von Staat, Wirtschaft und Gesellschaft Lateinamerikas* 25 (1988): 33–59; William O. Henderson, *The Rise of German Industrial Power, 1834–1914* (Berkeley, 1975), 23–108; Wolfgang Hardtwig, *Vormärz: Der monarchische Staat und das Bürgertum* (Munich, 1985), 106–72.

8. Hans-Ulrich Wehler, "Industrial Growth and Early German Imperialism," in Roger Owen and Bob Sutcliffe, eds., *Studies in the Theory of Imperialism* (London, 1972), 71–92.

9. Published materials on colonization organizations in I Hauptabteilung, Preussisches Staatsministerium (Rep. 90), Nr. 232, Geheimes Staatsarchiv Preussischer Kulturbesitz, Berlin; Jahresberichte des Hamburger Colonisationsvereins, 1851–1855, Akten des Bundestages, DB/28, vol. 1, Bundesarchiv, Aussenstelle Frankfurt; Franz Hugo Hesse, "Andeutungen über Mittel-Amerika und seine Zukunft," AA II Rep. 6, Nr. 3518, Bundesarchiv Merseburg (BAM); Hesse to Otto von Manteuffel, 30 Dec. 1852, 2.4.1., Abt. II, Nr. 5246 (AA III, Rep. 14, Nr. 534), BAM; Julio Castellanos Cambranes, "Aspectos del desarrollo socio-económico y político de Guatemala, 1868–1885, en base de materiales de archivos alemanes," *Política y sociedad* 3 (1977): 7–14; Herbert Schottelius, *Mittelamerika als Schauplatz deutscher Kolonisationsversuche, 1840–1865* (Hamburg, 1939); Schoonover, "German Penetration of Central America."

10. Thomas Schoonover, "Latin America," in James W. Cortada, ed., *Spain in the Nineteenth-Century World: Essays on Spanish Diplomacy, 1789–1898* (Westport, Conn., 1994), 113–30; Antonia Pi-Suner, *México y España durante le República Restaurada* (Mexico, 1985), 20–21; James W. Cortada, *Spain and the American Civil War: Relations at Mid-Century, 1855–1868* (Philadelphia, 1980); Cortada, *Two Nations over Time: Spain and the United States, 1776–1977* (Westport, Conn., 1978).

11. Langley, *Struggle for the American Mediterranean,* 25–106; Thomas Schoonover, "Imperialism in Middle America: United States Competition with Britain, Germany, and France, 1820s–1920s," in Rhodri Jeffreys-Jones, ed., *Eagle against Empire: American Opposition to European Imperialism, 1914–1982* (Provence, France, 1983), 41–58; David McCullough, *The Path between the Seas: The Creation of the Panama Canal, 1870–1914* (New York, 1971), 14–40.

12. John H. Coatsworth, "American Trade with European Colonies in the Caribbean and South America, 1790–1812", and George Rogers Taylor, "Agrarian Discontent in the Mississippi Valley preceding the War of 1812," in William A. Williams, ed., *The Shaping of American Diplomacy: Readings and Documents in American Foreign Relations,* 2 vols. (Chicago, 1970), 1:91–103; William A. Williams, *The Contours of American History* (Chicago, 1966), 225–342; Charles Vevier, "American Continentalism: An Idea of Expansion, 1845–1910," *American Historical Review* 65 (1960): 323–35; Lester Langley, *America and the Americas: The United States in the Western Hemisphere* (Athens, Ga., 1989), 53–81.

13. Langley, *Struggle for the American Mediterranean,* 51–106; Walter LaFeber, *The New Empire: An Interpretation of American Expansion, 1860–1898* (Ithaca, N.Y., 1963), 1–17; Hans-Ulrich Wehler, *Grundzüge der amerikanischen Aussenpolitik* (Frankfurt, 1983), 123–40, 145–54; LaFeber, *Inevitable Revolutions: The United States in Central America* (New York, 1983), 25–31; Thomas M. Leonard, *Central America and the United States: The Search for Stability* (Athens, Ga., 1991), 15–34.

14. Williams, *The Contours of American History,* 225–342; Emory Thomas, *The Confederate Nation, 1861–1865* (New York, 1979), 167–89; Peter Parrish, *The American Civil War* (New York, 1975), 398–401; Stanley Lebergott, "Why the South Lost: Commercial Purpose in the Confederacy, 1861–1865," *Journal of American History* 70 (1983): 58–74.

15. Cited in Vevier, "American Continentalism," 328.

16. Robert E. May, *The Southern Dream of Caribbean Empire, 1854–1861,* rev. ed. (Athens, Ga., 1989); Louis Martin Sears, *John Slidell* (Durham, N.C., 1925); Charles H. Brown, *Agents of Manifest Destiny: The Lives and Times of the Filibusters* (Chapel Hill, 1980); Thomas R. Hietala, *Manifest Design: Anxious Aggrandizement in Late Jacksonian America* (Ithaca, N.Y., 1985).

17. Thomas and Ebba Schoonover, "Foreign Relations and Bleeding Kansas in 1858," *Kansas Historical Quarterly* 42 (1976): 345–52.

18. Thomas and Ebba Schoonover, "Documents: Bleeding Kansas and Spanish Cuba in 1857, A Postscript," *Kansas History* 11 (1988/89): 240–42; Thomas Schoonover, "Intereses británicos en Costa Rica cerca 1857," *Estudios sociales centroamericanos* 6 (1973): 152–54.

19. Thomas Schoonover, *Dollars over Dominion: The Triumph of Liberalism in Mexican-United States Relations, 1861–1867* (Baton Rouge, 1978), introduction, conclusion.

20. Immanuel Wallerstein, *The Modern World-System III: The Second Era of Great Expansion of the Capitalist World-Economy, 1730s–1840s* (Orlando, 1988), 127–256; Wallerstein, *Historical Capitalism,* 47–72; Avery O. Craven, "Background Forces and the Civil War," in Bernard Mayo, ed., *The American Tragedy* (Hampden-Sydney, Va., 1959), 17–18; Raimundo Luraghi, *The Rise and Fall of the Plantation South* (New York, 1978), 146–52; Harold D. Woodman, *King Cotton and His Retainers: Financing and Marketing the Cotton Crop of the South, 1800–1925* (Lexington, Ky., 1968), 141–95.

21. Charles Beard, *The Industrial Revolution* (New York, 1901); Chase-Dunn, "Core-Periphery Relations," 159–76; Bob Sutcliffe, "Imperialism and Industrialization in the Third World," in Owen and Sutcliffe, eds., *Studies in the Theory of Imperialism,* 171–92.

22. James G. Randall and David Donald, *The Civil War and Reconstruction,* 2d ed. (Lexington, Mass., 1969), 357–58; Richard van Alstyne, *The Rising American Empire* (Chicago, 1960), 147–69; Vevier, "American Continentalism"; May, *The Southern Dream of Caribbean Empire,* esp. 217–49; Schoonover, *Dollars over Dominion,* 27, 31–35, 81–82; José Augustín Quintero to Robert M. T. Hunter, 20 August 1861, Hugh McLeod, "Memorandum [addressed to Quintero] on the True Route of the Pacific Rail Road for the Confederate States," n.d., Records of the Confederate States of America, Library of Congress, vol. 8; Beringer et al., *Why the South Lost the Civil War;* Jones, *Confederate Strategy from Shiloh to Vicksburg,* 16–32; Coulter, *The Confederate States of America.*

23. Schoonover, *The United States in Central America,* chap. 1 and appendix.

24. Thomas, *The Confederate Nation,* 167–89; Frank Vandiver, "Jefferson Davis and Confederate Strategy," in Bernard Mayo, ed., *The American Tragedy,* 19–32.

25. May, *The Southern Dream of Caribbean Empire,* 239–44; Gavin Wright, *The Political Economy of the Cotton South* (New York, 1978), xii, 7–8, 92–98.

26. Frank L. Owsley, *King Cotton Diplomacy: Foreign Relations of the Confederate States of America* (Chicago, 1931), 1–51; Gordon H. Warren, "The King Cotton Theory," in Alexander DeConde, ed., *Encyclopedia of American Foreign Policy,* 3 vols. (New York, 1978), 2:515–20; William Woodruff, *The Struggle for World Power, 1500–1980* (London, 1981); Schoonover, *The United States in Central America,* chap. 1 and appendix. Vandiver, "Jefferson Davis and Confederate Strategy" is an example of passive acknowledgment of world forces that are then subordinated to Confederate history, especially its military history.

27. Owsley, *King Cotton Diplomacy,* 20–25; Warren, "The King Cotton Theory"; Steven Hahn, "Class and State in Postemancipation Societies: Southern Planters in Comparative Perspective," *American Historical Review* 95 (1990): 75–98.

28. Michael H. Hunt, *Ideology and U.S. Foreign Policy* (New Haven, 1987), 171.

29. Seward, Senate speech, 11 March 1850, quoted in Williams, ed., *The Shaping of American Diplomacy,* 1:314.

30. Seward, St. Paul, Minnesota speech, 18 Sept. 1860, quoted in Williams, ed., *The Shaping of American Diplomacy,* 1:314.

31. Ernest N. Paolino, *The Foundations of the American Empire: William Henry Seward and U.S. Foreign Policy* (Ithaca, N.Y., 1973), 27–28; LaFeber, *The American Age,* 131–32.

32. LaFeber, *The New Empire,* 24–32; Paolino, *The Foundations of the American Empire,* 1–40; Vevier, "American Continentalism"; Schoonover, *Dollars over Dominion,* xvi–xviii, 56–59; Thomas Schoonover, "Black Colonization in Mexico and Central America during the Civil War: Foreign Relations and Imperialism," *Pacific Historical Review* 49 (1980): 607–20.

33. Walt Whitman, "A Broadway Pageant," in *Walt Whitman: The Complete Poems,* Francis Murphy, ed. (Baltimore, 1975), 273; Leonard P. Curry, *Blueprint for Modern America: Non-military Legislation of the First Civil War Congress* (Nashville, 1968), 244–52; Schoonover, *Dollars over Dominion,* xiii–xiv, 9–11.

34. Napoleon III to Forey, 3 July 1862, quoted in Alfred H. Hanna and Kathryn A. Hanna, *Napoleon III and Mexico: American Triumph over Monarchy* (Chapel Hill, 1971), 79–80; Tom Kemp, *Economic Forces in French History* (London, 1971), 173–78; Allen, *France in Central America;* G. de Sibourg to MAE, 15 April, 21 May 1854, CCC, Panama, vol. 1, AMAE; Félix Belly, *Percement de l'isthme de Panama par le canal de Nicaragua* (Paris, 1858), 121–57; Stanley J. Pincetl, Jr., "France and the Clayton Bulwer Treaty of 1850," *Annales* 45 (1968): 167–94; Henry Blumenthal, *France and the United States: Their Diplomatic Relations, 1789–1914* (Chapel Hill, 1970), 66–67.

35. Phelan, "Pan-Latinism," 279–98; Hanna and Hanna, *Napoleon III and Mexico;* Arnold Blumberg, *The Diplomacy of the Mexican Empire, 1863–1867* (Philadelphia, 1971), 107–34; Schoonover, *Dollars over Dominion,* 277–83.

36. Schoonover, "Latin America"; Jerónimo Bécker, *Historia de las relaciones exteriores de España durante el siglo XIX,* 3 vols. (Madrid, 1924–26), 2:471–79, 513–19; Pi-Suner, *México y España,* 20–21; Robert W. Frazer, "The Role of the Lima Congress, 1864–1865, in the Development of Pan-Americanism," *Hispanic American Historical Review* 29 (1949): 319–48; Schoonover, *Dollars over Dominion,* 61–65, 75–77; Cortada, *Spain and the American Civil War;* Thomas G. Powell, "Spain and Mexico," in *The Iberian-American Connection: Implications for U.S. Foreign Relations,* edited by Howard J. Wiarda, (Boulder, 1986), 253–92; Mark J. van Aken, *Pan-Hispanism: Its Origin and Development to 1866* (Berkeley, 1959), 50–58.

37. Schoonover, "The French in Middle America"; Schoonover, "Imperialism in Middle America."

38. Guy P. Palmade, *Capitalisme et capitalistes français au XIXe siècle* (Paris, 1961), 196–98; Joachim Kuhn, "Napoleon III und der Nicaraguakanal," *Historische Zeitschrift* 208 (1969): 295–319; F. L. Hardy to MAE, 1 May 1862, CCC, Guat., vol. 7, AMAE; unsigned report, 24 Feb. 1863, Affaires divers politiques, carton 2, folder, Affaires coloniales belgiques, AMAE; Edward Loos to Napoleon III, 18 June 1863, Analysis of the Loos dispatch, July

1863, Mémoires et Documents, Amér., vol. 68, AMAE; Blumenthal, *France and the United States,* 79–91; Marvin R. Zahniser, *Uncertain Friendship: American-French Diplomatic Relations through the Cold War* (New York, 1975), 127–47; Schoonover, "Black Colonization."

39. Schoonover, "Metropole Rivalry in Central America"; Schoonover, "Imperialism in Middle America"; Langley, *Struggle for the American Mediterranean,* 25–106.

40. Schoonover, *Dollars over Dominion,* 154–57, 192–202.

41. Schoonover, *Dollars over Dominion,* 174–76, 277–80.

42. Thomas Schoonover, "Mexican Affairs and the Impeachment of President Andrew Johnson," *The East Tennessee Historical Society's Publication* 46 (1974): 76–93.

43. Langley, *Struggle for the American Mediterranean,* 25–106; Schoonover, "Metropole Rivalry in Central America"; Schoonover, "Latin America"; Schoonover, *Dollars over Dominion,* 251–83.

44. Eduard Delius to Foreign Ministry, 6 Aug. 1866, Rep. 77, Tit. 226, Nr. 118, Band 2, BAM; Tulio von Bülow, "Sobre el proyecto de base naval alemana en 1868," *Revista de los Archivos Nacionales* 7 (1943): 147–49; Arthur Morrell to William H. Seward, 8 May 1868, enclosing Friedrich Wilhelm Franz Kinderling to J. Friedrich Lahmann, 20 April 1868, Lahmann to Julio Volio, 1 May 1868, Volio to Lahmann, 6 May 1868, U.S. Department of State, *Papers Relating to the Foreign Relations of the United States, 1868* (Washington: GPO, 1869), pt. 2; Kinderling to Royal Navy High Command, 22 May 1868, BAM, 2.4.1 Abt. II, Nr. 644 (A.A. II Rep. 6, Nr. 3573); "Franz Kinderling," MSg 1/1101, p. 185, Bundesarchiv, Militärarchiv, Freiburg. Helmuth Polakowsky, "Estación naval alemana en Costa Rica, 1883," *Revista de los Archivos Nacionales* 7 (1943): 56–65, denies Bismarck approved Kinderling's proposal.

"THE WHOLE FAMILY OF MAN"

Lincoln and the Last Best Hope Abroad

★ ★ ★

JAMES M. MCPHERSON

O n 1 December 1862, Abraham Lincoln delivered his second annual message to Congress. Today we would call it the State of the Union Address. The state of the Union in December 1862 was perilous in the extreme. The Confederate States of America stood proud and defiant as an independent nation whose existence mocked the pretense of union. Most European statesmen assumed that it was merely a matter of time until Lincoln would recognize the inevitable truth that the Union had ceased to exist and give up his bloody, quixotic effort to cobble it together again by force. At home, political opposition menaced the Lincoln administration's ability to continue the war. That opposition focused particularly on the Emancipation Proclamation, announced the preceding September and scheduled to go into effect on 1 January 1863. Lincoln had embraced emancipation both as a way to weaken the Confederacy by depriving it of slave labor and as a sweeping expansion of Union war aims. No longer would the North fight merely for restoration of the old Union—a Union where slavery flouted American ideals of liberty. Now the North would fight to give that Union "a new birth of freedom," as Lincoln put it almost a year later at Gettysburg.

By then the prospects of Union victory appeared much better than they had a year earlier. Nevertheless, Lincoln's eloquence in December 1862 shone as brightly as it did at Gettysburg. "Fellow-citizens, *we* cannot escape history," he told Congress—and the American people. "The fiery trial through which we pass, will light us down, in honor or dishonor, to the latest generation. . . . In *giving* freedom to the *slave,* we *assure* freedom to the free." For America, Lincoln insisted, this was the crossroads of history; this was where "we shall nobly save, or meanly lose, the last best, hope of earth."[1]

What did Lincoln mean? Why did he consider the Union—by which he meant the United States as one nation indivisible—to be the last best hope of earth? The last best hope for what? Like other political leaders of his generation, Lincoln was painfully aware of the fate of most republics through history. Some Americans alive in 1861 had seen two French republics rise and fall. Republican governments in Latin America seemed to come and go with bewildering frequency. The hopes of 1848 for the triumph of popular governments in Europe had been shattered by the counterrevolutions that brought a conservative reaction in the Old World. The brave experiment launched in Philadelphia four score and seven years before Lincoln spoke at Gettysburg seemed fragile indeed in this world bestrode by kings, emperors, czars, dictators, theories of aristocracy and inequality. Would the American experiment also succumb to the fate of most republics and collapse into tyranny or fall to pieces?

Not if Lincoln could help it. The central vision that guided him was preservation of the United States as a republic governed by popular suffrage, majority rule, and the Constitution. If the Confederate rebellion succeeded in its effort to sever the United States in two, popular government would be swept into the dustbin of history. The next time a disaffected minority lost a presidential election, as Southern-Rights Democrats had in 1860, that minority might invoke the Confederate precedent to proclaim secession. The United States would fragment into a dozen petty, squabbling fiefdoms. "The central idea pervading this struggle," said Lincoln in 1861, "is the necessity that is upon us, of proving that popular government is not an absurdity. We must settle this question now, whether in a free government the minority have the right to break up the government whenever they choose. If we fail it will go far to prove the incapability of the people to govern themselves." Nor was this a struggle "altogether for today," Lincoln told Congress in 1861. "It is for a vast future also." It "embraces more than the fate of these United States. It presents to the whole family of man, the question, whether a constitutional republic, or a democracy . . . can, or cannot maintain its territorial integrity." If it could not, the forces of reaction in Europe would smile in smug satisfaction at this proof of their contention that the upstart republic launched in 1776 could never survive—that government of, by, and for the people had indeed perished from the earth.[2]

The American sense of mission invoked by Lincoln—the idea that this new-world experiment was a beacon of freedom for oppressed peoples everywhere—is as old as the Mayflower Compact and as new as apparent American victory in the Cold War. "We shall be as a City upon a hill," said John Winthrop to his fellow Puritans as their ship approached Massachusetts Bay in 1630. "The eyes of all people are upon us." Thomas Jefferson addressed the Declaration of Independence to "the opinions of mankind." In 1783 George Washington congratulated his compatriots on the achievement of independence but warned them that "the eyes of the whole World are turned upon them." Like Lincoln four score years later, Washington declared that the impact of the American Revolution would not be confined "to the present age alone, for with our fate will the destiny of unborn Millions be involved."[3]

Most northern people in 1861 shared Lincoln's conviction that the fate of democratic government hung on the outcome of the Civil War. That passion sustained them through four years of the bloodiest war in the Western world between 1815 and 1914. "We must fight," insisted an Indianapolis newspaper two weeks after the firing on Fort Sumter, "because we *must*. The National Government has been assailed. The Nation has been defied. If either can be done with impunity neither Nation nor Government is worth a cent. . . . War is self preservation, if our form of

Government is worth preserving. If monarchy would be better, it might be wise to quit fighting, admit that a Republic is too weak to take care of itself, and invite some deposed Duke or Prince of Europe to come over here and rule us. But otherwise, *we must fight.*"[4]

None felt this sense of democratic mission more strongly than Union soldiers, who periled their lives for it. "I do feel that the liberty of the world is placed in our hands to defend," wrote a Massachusetts private to his wife in 1862, "and if we are overcome then farewell to freedom." A thirty-five-year-old Indiana sergeant agreed with a Connecticut corporal that if the United States, as "the beacon light of liberty & freedom for the human race" were to lose the war, "all the hope and confidence of the world in the capacity of men for self government will be lost." In 1863, on the second anniversary of his enlistment, a thirty-three-year-old Ohio private wrote in his diary that he had not expected the war to last so long, but no matter how much longer it took, it must be carried on "for the great principles of liberty and self government at stake, for should we fail, the onward march of Liberty in the Old World will be retarded at least a century, and Monarchs, Kings, and Aristocrats will be more powerful against their subjects than ever."[5]

Some foreign-born soldiers expressed such convictions with even greater intensity. In 1864 a forty-year-old Ohio corporal who had immigrated from England wrote to his wife explaining his decision to reenlist for a second three-year hitch: "If I do get hurt I want you to remember that it will be not only for my Country and my Children but for Liberty all over the World that I risked my life, for if Liberty should be crushed here, what hope would there be for the cause of Human Progress anywhere else?" And a thirty-three-year-old Irish-born carpenter, a private in the 28th Massachusetts Infantry of the famous Irish Brigade, rebuked both his wife in Boston and his father-in-law in Ireland for questioning his judgment in risking his life for the Lincoln administration's war aims. "This is the first test of a modern free government in the act of sustaining itself against internal enemys," he wrote almost in echo of Lincoln. "If it fails then the hopes of milions fall and the designs and wishes of all tyrants will succeed the old cry will be sent forth from the aristocrats of europe that such is the common lot of all republics. . . . Irishmen and their descendants have . . . a stake in [this] nation. . . . America is Irlands refuge Irlands last hope destroy this republic and her hopes are blasted."⁶

Perhaps it is not surprising that Americans both native and adopted felt this way. They had never hidden their self-proclaimed beacon light of freedom under a bushel basket. But did peoples of other lands share the belief in America's mission to show them the path upward from autocracy and oppression? For liberals, radicals, progressives, reformers, and revolutionaries of all stripes, the answer is yes. During the first century of its history as a nation, the United States did serve as a model for the European and Latin American "Left" that sought to reform or overthrow the *anciens régimes* in their own countries. During the debate that produced the British Reform Act of 1832, the London Working Men's Association pronounced "the Republic of America" to be a "beacon of freedom" for all mankind, while a British newspaper named *The Poor Man's Guardian* pointed to American institutions as "the best precedent and guide to the oppressed and enslaved people of England in *their* struggle for the RIGHT OF REPRESENTATION FOR EVERY MAN." In the 1840s, English Chartists praised "the bright luminary of the western hemisphere whose radiance will . . . light the whole world to freedom and happiness . . . [and triumph] over the dark fiends of despotism, vice, and wretchedness."⁷

In the preface to the twelfth edition of his monumental *Democracy in America,* written during the heady days of the 1848 uprisings in Europe, Alexis de Tocqueville urged the leaders of France's newly created Second Republic to study American institutions as a guide to "the approaching irresistible and universal spread of democracy throughout the world." When instead of democracy France got the Second Empire under Napoleon III, the liberal opposition to his regime looked to the United States for inspiration. "Many of the suggested reforms," wrote the historian of the French opposition, "would have remained utopic had it not been for the demonstrable existence of the United States and its republican institutions." Napoleon's interior minister noted sourly that "one would almost be tempted to think that there was a fixed determination or combination to offer the United States always as an example for everything."[8]

Anti-Americanism was the hobby of the European "Right" in those years, particularly in England. As a British radical newspaper expressed it in 1856, "to the oppressors of Europe, especially those of England, the [United States] is a constant terror, and an everlasting menace" because it stood as "a practical and triumphant refutation of the lying and servile sophists who maintain that without kings and aristocrats, civilized communities cannot exist."[9] This rhetoric undoubtedly overstates the case. But the sentiments it describes certainly existed among high Tories—and some not so high. Many of them expressed delight, at least in private, at the "immortal smash" of the dis-United States in 1861, which demonstrated "the failure of republican institutions in time of pressure." The Earl of Shrewsbury looked upon "the trial of Democracy and its failure" with pleasure. "I believe that the dissolution of the Union is inevitable, and that men before me will live to see an aristocracy established in America." The voice of the British Establishment, the *Times* of London, considered the downfall of "the American colossus" a good "riddance of a nightmare. . . . Excepting a few gentlemen of republican tendencies, we all expect, we nearly all wish, success to the Confederate cause."[10]

Several historians have cautioned us not to overgeneralize from such examples. A simple dichotomy between British liberals who admired American democracy and supported the Union and conservatives who detested both does considerable violence to historical reality. Several prominent members of the nobility and gentry sympathized with the Union. And the Conservative party, out of power during the years of the American Civil War, did not press for recognition of the Confederacy despite the presence of many southern sympathizers in its ranks. There were many pro-Confederate partisans in Prime Minister Palmerston's Whig party as well—but never enough to bring about the Confederacy's chief foreign-policy goal, diplomatic recognition by Britain.[11]

Nevertheless, most members of that minority of Englishmen who owned enough property to vote—and who were therefore represented in Parliament—probably would have welcomed the dissolution of the American republic. The foremost British champion of the Union, John Bright, explained to an American friend that "Our Govt is made up of men drawn from the aristocratic families . . . and from a natural instinct, it must be hostile to your greatness & to the permanence of your institutions." Bright's pro-Union colleague, Richard Cobden, may have exaggerated only slightly when he wrote in December 1861, at the time of the furor over the Union navy's seizure of Confederate envoys James Mason and John Slidell from the British ship *Trent,* that "three fourths of the House [of Commons] will be glad to find an excuse for voting for the dismemberment of the Great Republic."[12] When Sir John Ramsden, a Tory member of the House, expressed satisfaction that "the great republican bubble had burst," loud cheers broke forth from the back benches. The American minister to the Court of St. James, Charles Francis Adams, was not too far off the mark when he wrote in December 1862 that "the great body of the aristocracy and the commercial classes are anxious to see the United States go to pieces."[13]

We know much less about conservative attitudes toward the Civil War in other countries. What little we do know, however, finds conservatives outside of Britain expressing the same kind of satisfaction with the failure of democracy. The leading English-language newspaper in South Africa concluded in June 1861 that the "boasted republic" had "fallen asunder at the first touch, and added another to the many examples of the inefficiency of large republics to stand against popular passions." A year later, a royalist Spanish journal, the *Pansiemento español,* found it scarcely surprising that Americans were butchering each other, for that nation "was populated by the dregs of all the nations of the world. . . . Such is the real history of the one and only state in the world which has succeeded in constituting itself according to the flaming theories of democracy. The example is too horrible to stir any desire for emulation."[14]

In Paris, *La patrie,* a semiofficial organ for Napoleon III, stated with ill-concealed relish in August 1861 that "the work of George Washington has come to an end." Napoleon's foreign policy was the most pro-Confederate of any European power. If the emperor had been able to persuade Britain or Russia to go along, France would have offered mediation and diplomatic recognition of the Confederacy. The French liberal Edgar Quinet exaggerated only slightly when he wrote from exile in Switzerland in 1862 that Napoleon's purpose was "to weaken or destroy Democracy in the United States . . . because in order for Napoleonic ideas to succeed, it is absolutely indispensable that this vast republic disappear from the face of the earth."[15]

Whether or not Napoleon thought he could destroy republicanism in the United States, he undertook to do so in Mexico. That unhappy country experienced its own civil war in the 1860s between a reactionary alliance of the church and large landowners against followers of the republican liberal Benito Juárez. Under the pretext of collecting debts owed to French citizens, Napoleon sent an army of 35,000 men to Mexico to overthrow Juárez. Napoleon's main motive was to reestablish the French presence in the New World yielded by his uncle sixty years earlier when he had sold Louisiana to the United States. Napoleon was also quite willing to go along with his fellow emperor, Francis Joseph of Austria, whose younger brother, Ferdinand Maximilian, was at loose ends with little to do. Why not set him up as emperor of Mexico, thereby reclaiming at least part of the vast Spanish domain once ruled by the Hapsburgs? King Leopold of Belgium, Maximilian's father-in-law, had an additional purpose in mind. Describing the Lincoln administration as being characterized by "the most rank Radicalism," Leopold feared that if the North won the war, "America, in collaboration with Europe's revolutionaries, might undermine the very basis of the traditional social order of Europe." Therefore he strongly supported the installation of Maximilian as emperor of Mexico in 1864 "to raise a barrier against the United States and provide a support for the monarchical-aristocratic principle in the Southern states."[16]

While these emperors were fishing in troubled New World waters, the most autocratic of them all, Tsar Alexander of Russia, proved to be the Union's most steadfast friend. This friendship did not result from reasons of sentiment or ideology. Quite the contrary; no two regimes could have been farther apart in political philosophy and cultural values. Russo-American relations during the Civil War were a marriage of convenience founded on the self-interest of both parties: the Russian interest in a strong

United States as a counterweight to Britain, and the American dependence on Russia as a counterweight to French and British flirtation with recognition of the Confederacy. Russian opposition to mediation of the American conflict by the great powers gave the *coup de grâce* to that effort in November 1862. A year later, the Russian fleet visited American ports, staying for months, ostensibly as a good-will gesture but in reality as a way to prevent the British navy from bottling up Russian ships in their home ports during a period of tension over Russian suppression of an uprising of Polish nationalists.

Although ideology did not inhibit the strange-bedfellow comity between Russia and the United States, that does not mean ideology was absent from Russian perceptions of the war's meaning for democracy. The confidential dispatches of the Russian minister to the United States, Edouard de Stoeckl, to the Russian foreign minister, Prince Alexander Gorchakov, provide a fascinating glimpse of the crosscurrents and contradictions of realpolitik and ideology. Stoeckl had lived in the United States for twenty years before the war. He liked Americans and married one in 1856. But he fancied himself an aristocrat and enjoyed being addressed as "Baron," though he had no title of nobility. He supported the Union cause but considered it hopeless until almost the end of the war. He detested democracy and regarded the Civil War as proof of its failure. "The republican form of government, so much talked about by the Europeans and so much praised by the Americans, is breaking down," he wrote to Prince Gorchakov with apparent satisfaction in December 1863. "What can be expected from a country where men of humble origin are elevated to the highest positions?" He meant Lincoln, whose abilities Stoeckl held in low regard. "This is democracy in practice, the democracy that European theorists rave about," continued Stoeckl. "If they could only see it at work they would cease their agitation and thank God for the government which they are enjoying."[17]

Those theorists whom Stoeckl sneered at—that is, European liberals and radicals—viewed the American Civil War with alarm. Perhaps the reactionaries were right, after all, and the downfall of Lincoln's last best hope of earth would prove the absurdity of everything they believed in.

French liberals, wrote one of them in 1861, "feel somehow humbled and certainly very distressed by this deplorable Civil War" because "it may very well bring about the failure of a society" held up by liberals as the "defenders of right and humanity."[18]

Nevertheless, republican deputies in the French Assembly declared hopefully in 1862 that the war's outcome would prove "that the most grave crisis cannot be disastrous to a people who do not separate democracy and liberty." In England Bright described "that free country and that free government [which] has had a prodigious influence upon freedom in Europe and in England" as now fighting with their back to the wall as the "advocates and defenders of freedom and civilization." The famous economist and political philosopher John Stuart Mill, who fervently favored the Union cause, believed that Confederate success "would be a victory for the powers of evil which would give courage to the enemies of progress and damp the spirits of its friends all over the civilized world. . . . [The American war] is destined to be a turning point, for good and evil, of the course of human affairs."[19]

While this destiny hung in the balance, Bright and Mill and other liberals in Britain and France gave speeches, wrote editorials, and organized meetings to endorse the Union cause and to bring pressure on their respective governments to prevent any kind of recognition of, or support for, the Confederacy. The question arises, How important were these efforts? How much influence did they have? It is true that European governments never did recognize the Confederacy or intervene to break the Union blockade, despite the cotton shortage that put hundreds of thousands of textile workers out of work by 1862. But was this nonintervention the consequence of public pressure? After all, much of the pro-Union population in Britain and France was disfranchised or politically powerless. And, as I have written elsewhere, "considerations of power and national self-interest, more than of ideology and public opinion, ultimately determined European policy toward the Civil War."[20] Palmerston and Napoleon both leaned toward the Confederacy in their sentiments, yet they backed off from the brink of recognizing the Confederacy as an independent nation. Considerations of realpolitik rather than their personal attitudes or the influence of public opinion either for or against the Union cause were indeed uppermost in determining the neutrality of these countries toward the American conflict.

But we must not go so far as to deny the impact of public opinion altogether. Diplomatic historians have in recent years increasingly emphasized the importance of internal political, social, cultural, and ideological factors in shaping the context in which governments determine their foreign policy. No intelligent observer today would deny, for example, that domestic concerns strongly influence American foreign policy. These factors are, of course, more important in a democratic polity than they were in European countries in the 1860s. Nevertheless, governments such as those of Britain and France could not entirely ignore domestic opinion in formulating their policies toward the American war.

This was especially true with regard to slavery. Having abolished the institution in their colonies, European countries now prided themselves on their antislavery stance. Autocratic Russia had ended serfdom in 1861. Britain regarded itself as the world's policeman against the slave trade. Even Tories professed distaste for the South's peculiar institution. Confederate envoys in Britain seeking diplomatic recognition in 1861 acknowledged ruefully that "the public mind here is entirely opposed to the Government of the Confederate States of America on the question of slavery. . . . The sincerity and universality of this feeling embarrass the Government in dealing with the question of our recognition." Lincoln recognized this truth when he said privately in January 1862: "I cannot imagine that any European power would dare to recognize and aid the Southern Confederacy if it became clear that the Confederacy stands for slavery and the Union for freedom."[21]

The problem was that in the first seventeen months of the war, the Union did not stand for freedom. This perplexed and even embittered some Europeans, who failed to understand the constitutional and political constraints that hindered Lincoln from turning the war for Union into a war against slavery. Since "the North does not proclaim abolition and never pretended to fight for anti-slavery," asked perturbed Englishmen in September 1861, how "can we be fairly called upon to sympathize so warmly with the Federal cause?"

This attitude helps explain the ambivalent and much-debated position of British workingmen toward the American war. The historiography of that question has gone through a sort of Hegelian dialectic of thesis, antithesis, and synthesis. The traditional interpretation portrayed workingmen as sympathizing with the Union as the great symbol of progressivism and equal rights. This sympathy was said to overcome even the self-interest of workers in the textile industry, whose livelihood depended on slave-grown cotton and who suffered grievous hardships by the blockade of southern ports. This interpretation cites many meetings of unemployed textile workers who passed resolutions favoring the Union and warning their own government against intervention in behalf of the Confederacy, even to get cotton. Contemporary observers seemed to support this interpretation. In 1862 Henry Hotze, a Confederate journalist in London, acknowledged that "the Lancashire operatives" are the only "class which as a class continues actively inimical to us. . . .They look upon us, and . . . upon slavery as the author and source of their present miseries." And Adams maintained that the British lower classes "sympathize with us" because they "see in the convulsion in America an era in the history of the world, out of which must come in the end a general recognition of the right of mankind to the produce of their labor."[22]

A generation ago, however, the inevitable revisionism that allows no historical interpretation to rest easy came along to challenge this thesis. Most Lancashire textile workers, according to revisionists, actually favored the Confederacy—or at least favored British intervention to break the blockade and get cotton, which amounted to the same thing. All those meetings and their resolutions favoring the Union, according to this Hegelian antithesis, were gotten up by middle-class radical ideologues, not by the workers themselves.[23]

What explains these conflicting interpretations? Is there any way to resolve them? The answer lies in slavery—the institution that explains many things about the American Civil War. So long as the North fought merely for restoration of the Union—a Union with slavery—many labor leaders, and presumably their constituents, saw little moral difference between North and South. Therefore why not recognize Confederate independence, end the war, and thereby put an end to unemployment and misery in the textile district? In a typical editorial, a British labor newspaper declared in October 1861: "Now that it is clear that the Northerners in America are not fighting for the emancipation of the slaves, we are relieved from any moral consideration in their favor, and as the Southerners are not worse than they are, why should we not get cotton? . . . If the North, in blockading the Southern ports, had had emancipation in view, we might have seen the sacred cause of free labour was on their side." Since this is not the case, "why should we starve any longer?"[24]

Lincoln recognized the force of this question. Years earlier he had noted that "the monstrous injustice of slavery . . . deprives our republican example of its just influence in the world—enables the enemies of free institutions, with plausibility, to taunt us as hypocrites." In September 1862, Lincoln agreed with a delegation of antislavery clergymen that "emancipation would help us in Europe, and convince them that we are incited by something more than ambition." When he said this, Lincoln had already decided to issue a proclamation of emancipation and was only awaiting a Union military victory to announce it.[25]

That victory came a few days later, at Antietam. But to Lincoln's disappointment and puzzlement, the Emancipation Proclamation did not immediately transform critical European opinion. The preliminary nature of the edict that Lincoln issued on 22 September 1862, the exemption of Unionist areas, and the justification of the proclamation on grounds of military necessity, not morality and justice, gave European cynics a field day. Many regarded it as a Yankee trick to encourage a slave insurrection and undertaken not from moral conviction but as a desperate measure to destroy the Confederacy from within because Union armies could not defeat it from without. The British chargé d'affaires in Washington branded the proclamation as "cold, vindictive, and entirely political." Foreign

Secretary Lord John Russell, who had previously withheld sympathy from the Union because it did *not* act against slavery, now perversely pronounced the Emancipation Proclamation a vile encouragement to "acts of plunder, of incendiarism, and of revenge."[26] Choosing not to understand why Lincoln, under the Constitution, had to exempt the loyal border states and Union-occupied portions of the Confederacy, the London *Spectator* sneered that "the principle asserted is not that a human being cannot own another, but that he cannot own him unless he is loyal to the United States." Even the most radical British labor newspaper lamented that "Lincoln offers freedom to the negroes over whom he has no control, and keeps in slavery those other negroes within his power. Thus he associates his Government with slavery by making slaveholding the reward to the planters of rejoining the Old Union."[27]

But in the end, all of this sound and fury signified little. Most British liberals understood the enormous portent of the Emancipation Proclamation. A friendly London newspaper pronounced it "the great fact of the war . . . a gigantic stride in the paths of Christian and civilized progress—the turning point in the history of the American commonwealth—an act only second in courage and probable results to the Declaration of Independence." When Lincoln, contrary to the prediction of some hostile Europeans, followed through with the final Emancipation Proclamation on 1 January 1863, many former skeptics became true believers. Implicitly responding to criticisms of the preliminary proclamation, Lincoln this time pronounced emancipation to be "an act of justice" as well as of military necessity and enjoined freed slaves to refrain from violence.[28]

Even though the final proclamation exempted one quarter of the slaves, Lincoln had nevertheless announced a new war aim. Thenceforth the Union army became officially an army of liberation. If the North won the war, slavery would exist no more. As recognition of this truth began to dawn across the Atlantic during January and February 1863, a powerful pro-Union reaction set in, especially in England. Huge meetings roared their approval of emancipation and endorsement of the Union cause. Young Henry Adams, secretary to his father at the American legation in London, reported that "the Emancipation Proclamation has done more for us here than all our former victories and all our diplomacy. It has created an almost convulsive reaction in our favor."[29]

Many of these mass meetings were organized by workingmen. That gives us the Hegelian synthesis which resolves the question of their position on the American war: once emancipation became a war aim, they were solidly pro-Union. Quotations could be piled up endlessly to demonstrate the point, but one workingman's speech at a rally in Manchester on 24 February 1863 will have to stand for all the rest. The people of the North, he said in the paraphrased words of a reporter, were "not merely contending for themselves, but for the rights of the unenfranchised of this and every other country. If the North succeed, liberty [will] be stimulated and encouraged in every country on the face of the earth; if they fail, despotism, like a great pall, [will] envelop all our political and social institutions."[30]

This upswelling of public support for Union and emancipation did not determine British foreign policy. But it certainly helped shape the context in which such determination was made. Contemporary observers believed that it killed whatever lingering chance might have existed for British recognition of the Confederacy. Charles Francis Adams, no sentimentalist, said that it would "annihilate all agitation for recognition." Cobden reported in February 1863 that one of the largest of the pro-Union mass meetings, at Exeter Hall in London, "has had a powerful effect on our newspapers and politicians. It has closed the mouths of those who have been advocating the side of the South. Recognition of the South, by England, whilst it bases itself on Negro slavery, is an impossibility." In France a year later, at a time when Napoleon was toying with the idea of recognizing the Confederacy in return for Confederate recognition of his puppet, Maximilian, in Mexico, twelve prominent French citizens of Tours addressed a public letter to Slidell, telling him bluntly: "It is useless to make any appeal to the people of France. It may be to our interest to support you. There may be strong material and political reasons for a close alliance between us, but as long as you maintain and are maintained by slavery, we cannot offer you our alliance. On the contrary, we believe and expect you will fail!"[31]

The Confederacy did fail. The last best hope of earth for democracy did not perish from the earth but experienced a new birth of freedom whose impact was felt abroad with telling effect. From Spanish republicans in 1865 came congratulations to "a people democratically governed" who have "carried to its close the greatest enterprise in history." The Italian patriot and revolutionary Guiseppe Mazzini blessed the northern people, who "have done more for us in four years than fifty years of teaching, preaching and writing from all your European brothers have been able to do." None other than Karl Marx declared that "as in the eighteenth century the American War of Independence sounded the tocsin for the European middle class, so in the nineteenth century, the American Civil War sounded it for the working class."[32]

It is scarcely surprising that European liberals and radicals indulged in an orgy of mutual congratulations at the news of Union victory. More impressive, perhaps, and more illustrative of the impact of that victory, were the responses of conservatives. A British Tory in the House of Commons, a critic of American culture and democracy, remarked sourly to an American acquaintance that he considered Union success a misfortune. "I had indulged the hope that your country might break up into two or perhaps more fragments. I regard the United States as a menace to the whole civilized world." A Tory colleague spelled out the menace as "the beginning of an Americanizing process in England. The new Democratic ideas are gradually to find embodiment."[33] Most remarkable of all was the reaction of Stoeckl, who despised democracy, had considered the Civil War proof of its failure, and had predicted Confederate victory until almost the eve of Appomattox. When the outcome proved him wrong, he ate humble pie in a dispatch to Prince Gorchakov. By "an irresistible strength of the nation at large," wrote Stoeckl, "this exceptional people, has given the lie to all predictions and calculations. . . . They have passed through one of the greatest revolutions of a century . . . and they have come out of it with their resources unexhausted, their energy renewed . . . and the prestige of their power greater than ever."[34]

The consequences of this triumph of democracy were more than symbolic. It encouraged liberals in Britain who wanted to expand voting rights there. For almost four years, they had endured the taunts and jibes of Tories who pointed to the American "smashup" as evidence of democracy's failure. "Our opponents told us that Republicanism was on trial," recalled Edward Beesly, a liberal professor of political economy at University College London, in 1865. "They insisted on our watching what they called its breakdown. They told us that it was for ever discredited in England. Well, we accepted the challenge. We staked our hopes boldly on the result. . . . Under a strain such as no aristocracy, no monarchy, no empire could have supported, Republican institutions have stood firm. It is we, now, who call upon the privileged classes to mark the result. . . . A vast impetus has been given to Republican sentiments in England."[35]

A two-year debate in Parliament, in which the American example figured prominently, led to enactment of the Reform Bill of 1867, which nearly doubled the eligible electorate and enfranchised a large part of the British working class for the first time. With this act, the world's most powerful nation took a long stride toward democracy. It is an oversimplification to attribute this achievement mainly to Union victory in the Civil War. But it is probably no exaggeration to say that if the North had lost the war, thereby confirming Tory opinions of democracy and confounding the liberals, the Reform Bill would have been delayed for years.[36]

If the triumph of democracy in Britain was an indirect result of the American Civil War, the triumph of Juárez and republicanism in Mexico was a direct result. The United States sent fifty thousand veteran troops to Texas after Appomattox, while Secretary of State William H. Seward pressed the French to pull their troops out of Mexico. Napoleon did so in 1866, whereupon the republican forces under Juárez regained control of the country, captured Maximilian, and executed him in 1867, leaving his wife, Carlotta, to wander insane over the face of Europe for sixty years. Three years after the fall of Maximilian, Napoleon himself lost his throne, an event attributed by the historian of his liberal opposition in part to the example of triumphant republicanism in the United States five years earlier.[37]

This is pushing things too far; the birth of France's third republic was a consequence of French defeat in the Franco-Prussian War, not of Union victory in the American Civil War. But perhaps it is more than coincidence that within five years of that Union victory, the forces of liberalism had expanded the suffrage in Britain and toppled emperors in Mexico and France. And it is also more than coincidence that after the abolition of slavery in the United States, the abolitionist forces in the two remaining slave societies in the western hemisphere, Brazil and Cuba, stepped up their campaign for emancipation, which culminated in success two decades later. If he had lived, Lincoln would have been gratified by the statement of a Brazilian intellectual in 1871, referring to his government's commitment to emancipation, that he rejoiced "to see Brazil receive so quickly the moral of the Civil War in the United States."[38]

Lincoln would applaud even more the essay written in 1993 by a seventeen-year-old girl from Texas in a contest sponsored by the Huntington Library in connection with its recent exhibit on Lincoln. This girl, whose forebears immigrated from India thirty years ago, wrote that "if the United States was not in existence today, I would not have the opportunity to excel in life and education. The Union was preserved, not only for the people yesterday, but also for the lives of today."[39] In 1861 Lincoln said that the struggle for the Union involved not just "the fate of these United States" but of "the whole family of man." It was a struggle "not altogether for today" but "for a vast future" as well. Lincoln's words resonate today with as much relevance as they did six score and thirteen years ago.

QUESTION: Would British and French recognition of the Confederacy have made a difference? And isn't it true that the Union navy was so strong that it would have stopped any intervention by Britain and France if those countries had tried to get involved in the Civil War?

ANSWER: Some people have sometimes suggested, in fact, that it would not have mattered if Britain and France had recognized the Confederacy; the Union did develop a very strong navy as the war went on. They say, essentially, sticks and stones may break my bones, but bad words can never hurt me. That is, bad words being diplomatic recognition. So what? But I think it is more than a "so what" question. If we consider two examples, one from a previous century and one from our own time, I think we can see the significance of recognition. The French assistance to the Americans in the Revolution was preceded by French recognition of the American nation. Recognition is an important first step toward something more important. In the case of the Revolution, the French followed up recognition with significant military and naval aid. British and French recognition of the Confederacy probably would not have led to the same kind of military and naval aid. But it would have enhanced the ability of the Confederates to sell bonds and obtain loans in Britain, using their cotton as collateral. Further, if the United States had responded to such recognition of the Confederacy by breaking diplomatic relations with Britain and France, which it might well have done, that would have elevated the level of tension between the Union and Britain back to the point where it had been in November 1861, at the time of the "*Trent* Affair," when many people expected the crisis to end in war. A war between Britain and the United States would have caused such a diversion of Union military resources that it might well have permitted the Confederacy to obtain its independence.

To take the twentieth-century example, when the Baltic nations Latvia, Estonia, and Lithuania were hoping to achieve their independence from the Soviet Union in 1991, they worked very hard to achieve diplomatic recognition by European countries and the United States. Once the United States did recognize them as independent nations, independence became a reality. That act became sticks and stones. Now, that exact parallel may not apply in the case of the British and French in 1862. But recognition would have been a significant moral victory, and perhaps something more, for the Confederacy.

To sum up my response, it is perfectly true that the longer the war went on and the stronger the Union military became, the less danger there was for the North that European recognition of the Confederacy would have made a difference. The real danger existed in the first half of the war, and I think it might have made a difference at that stage.

QUESTION: What about the impact of the news of the Battle of Gettysburg on British and French opinion about the Civil War? Had the Confederates won that battle, would it have made a difference?

ANSWER: Yes, I think it would have reopened the issue of recognition. In fact, the issue had already been reopened in the British Parliament in the summer of 1863 in response to continuing Union military failures—especially the Union loss at the Battle of Chancellorsville and the apparent failure of General Grant to make any headway during the spring of 1863 in his campaign to take Vicksburg. A number of members of Parliament had been in consultation with the French government and came back to England and offered a motion in Parliament, in the latter part of June 1863, for recognition of the Confederacy. The motion did not get very far at the time, partly because of the somewhat maverick character of the members of Parliament who promoted it and partly because of British suspicions, which were well justified, that the French were behind the initiative. If the Battle of Gettysburg had come out differently, I am inclined to believe that the effort might have gained some momentum. It might have been interpreted as one more sign of what most Europeans thought anyhow—that sooner or later the North would have to realize that it could not win this war. It might have been the final nail in the coffin.

QUESTION: What accounts for the failure of "king cotton" diplomacy? How could so many Confederate leaders make the gross miscalculation that king cotton would give them the leverage to win European support?

ANSWER: Alexander Stephens, the vice president of the Confederacy, later claimed that he had advocated a policy of shipping cotton out as fast as possible in 1861 and storing it somewhere in Europe as collateral against European loans to buy arms, ammunition, and equipment for the Confederacy. Stephens complained that instead of following his advice, the Confederacy had done just the opposite—it basically embargoed cotton exports in 1861, hoping that the resulting shortage of cotton in Europe would put pressure on the British to intervene in the Civil War.

I have always been very skeptical that Stephens was that prescient in 1861. Furthermore, even if the Confederacy had tried to follow Stephens's advice, how would they have done it? Where were they going to get the ships to send all that cotton abroad, unless the British sent ships over to get the cotton and break the Union blockade? Would the British have done this, knowing that it would almost certainly result in war with the Union? And how sensible would it have been to send all that cotton over when there was already a glut of cotton in Europe? It would have driven the price of cotton down. How would the Confederacy have gotten much money for it?

So, although in retrospect it looks like it was a gross miscalculation for Confederate leaders to have counted on cotton, I am not at all sure that the plan was as ill advised as it appears today. We need to realize that the Confederates had no way of knowing that there was such a surplus of cotton in Europe at the time. Not all of that surplus was in raw cotton, by the way. Part of it was in an inventory of cloth, since the factories had run at full tilt in 1859, 1860, and 1861 to turn all that raw cotton into cloth. So I do not think it was as much blundering and shortsightedness on their part as it was a case of bad luck and a lack of information.

QUESTION: You mention that British Tories and European conservatives and aristocrats did not think much of Lincoln, his humble origins, and his bumbling leadership. Did they change their minds near the end of the war? And if they did change their minds, was it only because he was assassinated and became a martyr?

ANSWER: For the most part, the attitude of British papers, such as the *Times* of London, which was notoriously arrogant and sneering toward Lincoln, and *Punch,* the British humor magazine, which carried some cartoons of Lincoln caricaturing him in the most negative and defaming sort of way, carried their hostile attitude toward Lincoln almost to the end of the war. By March and April 1865, it began to sink in even to some of the thickest skulls in England that maybe the Confederacy was going to go down the tubes, and that maybe Lincoln after all had shown some skill and determination in holding the country together and winning the war. But the big flip-flop did not come until after Lincoln's assassination. The best place to follow this is either in the *Times* editorials, which did a 180-degree turn, or in *Punch's* cartoons. When the news of the assassination reached Britain, *Punch* suddenly put a cartoon on its cover showing Britain mourning for Lincoln's death. This was a 180-degree reversal from the way Lincoln had been portrayed just a short time earlier. You can see the same change in William Gladstone, chancellor of the exchequer in the Palmerston ministry throughout the war. Gladstone had been one of the strongest pro-Confederate advocates during the war. Yet several years after the war, Gladstone, who had enjoyed a long and illustrious public career, said that supporting the Confederacy was the greatest mistake he had made in his whole political career, and that he could not understand, looking back at it now in the 1870s, how he could have been so blind! But 90 percent of this change in the image of Lincoln and the Union cause in Britain happened after 14 April 1865.

QUESTION: I am curious about United States relations with Russia during the war. Here you have friendly relations between a democratic society in the United States and an autocratic society in Russia. What kind of an impact did this have on British and French perceptions of, and policies toward, the American Civil War?

ANSWER: Great Britain and France had fought a war with Russia a half dozen years earlier—the Crimean War. There was still great tension between Britain and Russia at the time of the Civil War, partly now over the Polish question, partly over traditional balance-of-power conflicts and a variety of other matters that divided the two powers. So the Russians saw it as in their interest to cultivate cordial relations with the Union that might later be reciprocated should there ever be a showdown with Great

Britain. Probably the show of friendship by the Russians for the Union did help to put a brake on those in the British and French governments who wanted to offer some support to the Confederacy. In November 1862, the British cabinet held an important meeting to decide whether or not to go along with French pressure to offer mediation in the Civil War, and, if mediation was not accepted, to offer diplomatic recognition to the Confederacy. They tried to get Russia and the other major European powers, Austria and Prussia, to go along. When Russia refused to do so, the British backed out, even though Napoleon still wanted to go ahead without Russia. So I think that in this particular instance, as well as in a more general sense, the friendly posture of Russia toward the Union may have helped discourage in some degree European intervention.

QUESTION: Did Brazil and Cuba offer the Confederacy any help as a way of preserving their own slave systems?

ANSWER.:   These countries did not offer much aid to the Confederacy. Of course, Cuba was a Spanish colony then, so it was up to Spain to make policy for Cuba regarding the Civil War. To the extent that the Spanish paid attention to the Civil War, they tended to favor the Confederates. And it may be that a perception of the potential danger to the future of slavery in Cuba if the Confederacy lost its bid for independence influenced Spanish policy. Spanish authorities did permit Confederate blockade runners to operate out of Havana. I do not know of any Brazilian overtures to the Confederacy. It is interesting to note that after the war, several thousand ex-Confederates, feeling that they could not live under the northern occupation of the southern states, emigrated to Brazil. Most of them eventually came home. But some stayed, and their descendants live in Brazil to this day. Even though over the generations most of them intermarried with Brazilians, you can still go to parts of Brazil and find people named Jones and Smith, and, for all I know, Beauregard and Early!

QUESTION: How much attention did foreign nations pay to U.S. Reconstruction policy after the Civil War?

ANSWER: Great Britain and France paid some attention to Reconstruction, but not very much. The one society that did pay a lot of attention to Reconstruction policy was South Africa, which was a British colony at that time. The reason they paid such attention was because they had the same kind of question facing them as did the United States in trying to incorporate freed slaves into American society. The British, as a colonial power, also watched Reconstruction in regard to policies concerning some of their other nonwhite colonies, such as Jamaica, where there was, in fact, an uprising against British colonial rule by the black population in 1865, which was ruthlessly suppressed. So there was some attention paid to American racial policies during Reconstruction by British colonial administrators who were concerned about similar kinds of things themselves. But the level of interest and concern was much lower than it had been during the war.

QUESTION: Why do we always ignore the American Indians when we talk about Civil War diplomacy? Weren't they nations that conducted diplomatic relations with the Union and Confederacy? And isn't it true that while Lincoln was offering emancipation to the slaves, he was hanging Indians in Minnesota? And didn't the five so-called civilized tribes in the Indian territory, the Creeks, Chickasaws, Cherokees, Choctaws, and Seminoles, fight for the Confederacy?

ANSWER: Your question leaves a misleading impression. There was a Sioux uprising in Minnesota in August and September 1862 that caused the deaths of some 500 whites, mostly women and children. Angry Minnesotans tried the Indians and condemned 303 of them to death. But when Lincoln heard about this, he was appalled. He asked for the trial transcripts, personally reviewed them, and then commuted the sentences of all but 38 of the Indians. In other words, instead of Lincoln hanging the Indians, he offered commutation to almost 90 percent of them. He only allowed the execution of 38 Indians proven by the trial transcripts to have actually murdered someone. Just participating in an uprising, to Lincoln, did not justify the death penalty.

Regarding the other part of your question, it is true that the dominant elements in these five nations did support the Confederacy and even formed treaties of alliance with the Confederate nation. A Cherokee chief, Stand Watie, actually served as a Confederate general. But there were other Indians in Indian territory and elsewhere who fought on the Union side. And in the case of Cherokees who supported the Confederacy, many of them were of mixed blood and even slaveholders. One of the reasons that they supported the Confederacy was that they, too, held slaves.

I would emphasize, however, that Lincoln's attitudes about, and policy toward, Indians were secondary in the sense of his perceptions of the meaning and purpose of this war. Lincoln, for the most part, did not pay a lot of attention to the Indian question. He confessed that he was preoccupied with the war and did not have a lot of time to devote attention to Indian affairs.

QUESTION: Would you elaborate a little on your closing remarks? I think you quoted Lincoln and said that Lincoln's words are just as true today as when he uttered them six score and seven years ago, and that the United States is still today the guardian of democracy. Do you really think that this is true?

ANSWER: Actually, I said that Lincoln's words are as *relevant* today as they were during the Civil War. That is a slightly different thing from saying that his words are as true today as they were then. I would hope that the United States would live up to its professed ideals when it comes to international affairs. It is all too true that in many respects the United States, in the last fifty years or so, has not always stood in defense of the forces of democracy and progressivism. Quite the contrary, in many cases, especially in the Cold War. Perhaps one of the things that the end of the

Cold War will liberate us from—and I am not predicting that this will necessarily happen—is the felt necessity always to defend conservative and even reactionary regimes so long as they are perceived as defending capitalism and United States interests. No, I did not mean to say that Lincoln's words are as true today as they were when he spoke them. I did mean to say that I hope that they are as relevant today.

NOTES

1. Roy P. Basler, ed., *The Collected Works of Abraham Lincoln,* 9 vols. (New Brunswick, N.J., 1953–55), 5:537 [hereafter cited as *CWL*].

2. Tyler Dennett, ed., *Lincoln and the Civil War in the Diaries and Letters of John Hay* (New York, 1939), 19–20; *CWL,* 5:53, 4:426.

3. Quoted in Richard N. Current, "Lincoln, the Civil War, and the American Mission," in Cullom Davis et al., eds., *The Public and Private Lincoln: Contemporary Perspectives* (Carbondale, 1979), 140, 141.

4. *Indianapolis Daily Journal,* 27 April 1861.

5. Josiah Perry to Phebe Perry, 3 Oct. 1862, Josiah Perry Papers, Illinois State Historical Library, Springfield; Samuel McIlvaine to "Mother and Friends," 29 Sept. 1862, in *By the Dim and Flaring Lamps: The Civil War Diaries of Samuel McIlvaine,* ed. Clayton E. Cramer (Monroe, N.Y., 1990), 147; Robert Goodyear to Sarah Goodyear, 14 Feb. 1863, in Robert Goodyear Letters, United States Army Military History Institute, Carlisle Barracks, Pa.; Robert T. McMahan Diary, entry of 3 Sept. 1863, State Historical Society of Missouri, Columbia, Mo.

6. George H. Cadman to Esther Cadman, 6 March 1864, Cadman Papers, Southern Historical Collection, University of North Carolina, Chapel Hill; Peter Welsh to Mary Welsh, 3 Feb. 1863, Peter Welsh to Patrick Prendergast, 1 June 1863, in *Irish Green and Union Blue: The Civil War Letters of Peter Welsh,* ed. Laurence Frederick Kohl and Margaret Cosse Richard (New York, 1986), 65–66, 102.

7. Quoted in G. D. Lillibridge, *Beacon of Freedom: The Impact of American Democracy upon Great Britain 1830–1870* (Philadelphia, 1955), 5, 28, 40, 43.

8. Tocqueville, *Democracy in America,* 12th ed., new translation by George Lawrence, ed. J. P. Mayer (New York, 1969), xiii; Serge Gavronsky, *The French Liberal Opposition and the American Civil War* (New York, 1968), 11, 12.

9. Quoted in Lillibridge, *Beacon of Freedom,* 80.

10. William H. Russell to John Bigelow, 14 April 1861, in John Bigelow, *Retrospections of an Active Life,* 2 vols. (New York, 1909), 1:347; Earl of Shrewsbury quoted in Ephraim D. Adams, *Great Britain and the American Civil War,* 2 vols. (New York, 1925), 2:282; *Times*

quoted in Frank L. Owsley, *King Cotton Diplomacy: Foreign Relations of the Confederate States of America,* 2d ed., revised by Harriet C. Owsley (Chicago, 1959), 186.

11. See especially Wilbur D. Jones, "The British Conservatives and the American Civil War," *American Historical Review* 58 (1953): 527–43; and Joseph M. Hernon, Jr., "British Sympathies in the American Civil War: A Reconsideration," *Journal of Southern History* 33 (1967): 356–67.

12. Bright to John Bigelow, 3 January 1862, in Belle Becker Sideman and Lillian Friedman, eds., *Europe Looks at the Civil War* (New York, 1960), 129; Cobden to "Mr. Paulton," December 1861, in ibid., 91.

13. Ramsden quoted in Jay Monaghan, *Diplomat in Carpet Slippers: Abraham Lincoln Deals with Foreign Affairs* (Indianapolis, 1945), 116; Charles Francis Adams to Charles Francis Adams, Jr., 25 Dec. 1862, in Worthington C. Ford, ed., *A Cycle of Adams Letters, 1861–1865,* 2 vols. (Boston, 1920), 1:220–21. See also Donald Bellows, "A Study of British Conservative Reaction to the American Civil War," *Journal of Southern History* 51 (1985): 505–26; and Sheldon Vanauken, *The Glittering Illusion: English Sympathy for the Southern Confederacy* (Worthing, England, 1988).

14. *Cape Argus,* 11 June 1861; *Pansiemento español,* September 1862, quoted in Sideman and Friedman, eds., *Europe Looks at the Civil War,* 173–74.

15. *La patrie* and Quinet quoted in Gavronsky, *The French Liberal Opposition,* 58, 167.

16. King Leopold to Queen Victoria, 17 Oct. 1861, in Sideman and Friedman, eds., *Europe Looks at the Civil War,* 98; Leopold quoted in A. R. Tyrner-Tyrnauer, *Lincoln and the Emperors* (New York, 1962), 69, 109.

17. Albert A. Woldman, *Lincoln and the Russians* (Cleveland, 1952), 216–17.

18. *Revue des deux mondes,* 15 Aug. 1861, quoted in Sideman and Friedman, eds., *Europe Looks at the Civil War,* 81.

19. French deputies quoted in David H. Pinkney, "France and the Civil War," in Harold M. Hyman, ed., *Heard Round the World: The Impact Abroad of the Civil War* (New York, 1969), 116; Bright quoted in H. C. Allen, "Civil War, Reconstruction and Great Britain," in ibid., 96, 75; Mill quoted in Sideman and Friedman, eds., *Europe Looks at the Civil War,* 117–18.

20. James M. McPherson, *Ordeal by Fire: The Civil War and Reconstruction,* 2d ed. (New York, 1992), 218.

21. William L. Yancey and A. Dudley Mann to Robert Toombs, 21 May 1861, in James D. Richardson, comp., *A Compilation of the Messages and Papers of the Confederacy,* 2 vols. (Nashville, 1906), 2:37; Lincoln quoted in *The Reminiscences of Carl Schurz,* 3 vols. (New York, 1907–8), 2:309.

22. Hotze quoted in Frank J. Merli, *Great Britain and the Confederate Navy, 1861–1865* (Bloomington, Ind., 1965), 23; Charles Francis Adams to Charles Francis Adams, Jr., 25 Dec. 1861, in Ford, ed., *Cycle of Adams Letters,* 1:220–21.

23. Royden Harrison, "British Labor and the Confederacy," *International Review of Social History* 2 (1957): 78–96; Mary Ellison, *Support for Secession: Lancashire and the American Civil War* (Chicago, 1972).

24. *The Working Man,* 5 Oct. 1861, quoted in Philip S. Foner, *British Labor and the American Civil War* (New York, 1981), 27–28.

25. *CWL,* 2:255, 5:423.

26. Chargé d'affaires quoted in Brian Jenkins, *Britain & the War for the Union,* 2 vols. (Montreal, 1974–80), 2:141; Russell quoted in Howard Jones, *Union in Peril: The Crisis over British Intervention in the Civil War* (Chapel Hill, 1992), 187.

27. *Spectator,* 11 Oct. 1862, quoted in Jenkins, *Britain & War for Union,* 2:153; *Bee-Hive,* 11 Oct. 1862, quoted in Foner, *British Labor and the American Civil War,* 29.

28. *Morning Star,* 6 Oct. 1862, quoted in Allan Nevins, *War Becomes Revolution,* vol. 2 of *The War for the Union* (New York, 1960), 270; *CWL,* 6:30.

29. Adams to Charles Francis Adams, Jr., 23 Jan. 1863, in Ford, ed., *Cycle of Adams Letters,* 1:243.

30. Quoted in Foner, *British Labor and the American Civil War,* 52.

31. Ford, ed., *Cycle of Adams Letters,* 1:243; Cobden to Charles Sumner, 13 Feb. 1863, in Sideman and Friedman, eds., *Europe Looks at the Civil War,* 222; citizens of Tours quoted in ibid., 261–62.

32. Spanish republicans and Mazzini quoted in ibid., 274, 282; Marx quoted in R. Laurence Moore, *European Socialists and the American Promised Land* (New York, 1970), 7.

33. Sir Edward Bulwer-Lytton to John Bigelow, April 1865, quoted in Sideman and Friedman, eds., *Europe Looks at the Civil War,* 282; Hyman, ed., *Heard Round the World,* xi.

34. Stoeckl to Gorchakov, 14 April 1865, quoted in Woldman, *Lincoln and the Russians,* 256–59.

35. Quoted in H. C. Allen, "Civil War, Reconstruction, and Great Britain," in Hyman, ed., *Heard Round the World,* 73.

36. See the discussion in ibid., 49–83.

37. Gavronsky, *The French Liberal Opposition,* 13.

38. Harry Bernstein, "The Civil War and Latin America," in Hyman, ed., *Heard Round the World,* 323.

39. Reena Mathew, "One Set of Footprints," essay in author's possession.

CONTRIBUTORS

★ ★ ★

ROBERT E. MAY is a professor of history at Purdue University. He is the author of *The Southern Dream of a Caribbean Empire, 1854–1861* (1973), *John A. Quitman: Old South Crusader* (1985), and a number of scholarly articles that treat the politics and diplomacy of the Civil War era. His current project is an analytical study of the "filibuster" expeditions in the mid-nineteenth century.

HOWARD JONES is University Research Professor and Chair of the Department of History at the University of Alabama. A recipient of the John F. Burnum Distinguished Faculty Award for teaching and research, he is the author of several books, including *Union in Peril: The Crisis over British Intervention in the Civil War* (1992), a History Book Club Selection; *Mutiny on the Amistad: The Saga of a Slave Revolt and Its Impact on American Abolition, Law, and Diplomacy* (1987); and *To the Webster-Ashburton Treaty: A Study in Anglo-American Relations, 1783–1843* (1977). He is presently working on the Anglo-American crisis over the *Alabama* and a diplomatic history of the war years.

R. J. M. BLACKETT is a professor of history at Indiana University and editor of the *Indiana Magazine of History*. He is the author of *Building an Antislavery Wall: Black Americans in the Atlantic Abolitionist Movement 1830–1860* (1983), *Beating Against the Barriers: Biographical Essays in Nineteenth-Century Afro-American History* (1986), and *Thomas Morris Chester: Black Civil War Correspondent* (1989). He is currently working on a study of British working-class reactions to the American Civil War.

THOMAS SCHOONOVER is a professor of history at the University of Southwestern Louisiana. He is the author of *Dollars over Dominion: The Triumph of Liberalism in Mexican-United States Relations, 1861–1867* (1978) and *The United States in Central America, 1860–1911: Episodes of Social Imperialism and Imperial Rivalry in the World System* (1991). He is the editor of two books, *The Mexican Lobby: Matias Romero in Washington, 1861–1867* (1985) and *A Mexican View of America in the 1860s: A Foreign Diplomat Describes the Civil War and Reconstruction* (1991). His current work is on the French and Germans in Central America.

JAMES M. MCPHERSON teaches at Princeton University, where he is the George Henry Davis 1886 Professor of American History. He also served as Commonwealth Fund Lecturer at University College, London, in 1982. The author of ten books on the American Civil War and Reconstruction eras, McPherson won the Pulitzer Prize in History in 1989 for his book *Battle Cry of Freedom: The Civil War Era* (1988). His most recent book is *What They Fought For, 1861–1865* (1994).

INDEX

★ ★ ★

Hietala, Thomas R., 109
Hispanicism, 124
Hispanismo, 124
Hitler, Adolf, 23
Honduran Interoceanic Railroad, 109, 119
Honduras, 112, 115
Hooker, Joseph, 77
Hope, Alexander Beresford, 79
Hopewood, John Turner, 85
Hotze, Henry, Confederate propagandist, 57, 84, 85, 89, 142
Huse, Caleb, 10, 25n. 13

Immigrants, to United States, 1, 69, 73–74, 134
Index (London), 57, 88
India: and British fears of revolution, 55, 95; as source of cotton for Britain, 5, 82, 83, 85, 90, 92; mentioned, 1
Indians (United States), 154–55
International law, 3, 4, 8, 50, 62n. 3, 67n. 37, 75
Ireland, 55, 63n. 7, 89
Irish Brigade, 134
Ironclads, 50, 56, 59
Isabella II, queen of Spain, 101, 102
Italy, 16, 19, 105, 122, 146

Jackson, Andrew, 71, 72–73, 80, 87
Jamaica, 154
Japan, 116
Jay, John, 60
Jenkins, Brian, 86
Johnson, Andrew, 13, 121
Johnson, John, 83
Johnston, Joseph, 12
Jones, Archer, 125n. 3
Jordan, Donaldson, 71, 76, 90
Juárez, Benito, Mexican president and Liberal leader: and France, 14, 118, 120, 147; pro-Union policies of, 124–25; mentioned, 102, 117, 138

Kansas, 110
Kenner, Duncan F., 12
Kenner mission, 12
Kershaw, T. B., 80
Kilmarnock, Scotland, 91
King Cotton, 61. *See also* France: and dependence on southern cotton; Great Britain: and dependence on southern cotton; South: and cotton
Kinney, Henry L., 109
Korea, 116

Laird rams, 11, 26n. 16
Lancashire, 40, 69, 70, 73, 74, 81, 84, 88, 89, 90, 93, 142
Latinism, 124
Latvia, 149
Lee, Robert E., 12, 36–37, 38, 39, 40, 42, 48
Leopold II, king of Belgium, 24n. 3, 138
Lesseps, Ferdinand de, 122
Lewis, George Cornewall, British secretary for war, 30, 49–51, 59, 61, 67n. 37
Liberalism, 110
Liberals, British. *See* Great Britain: Liberals in
Liberals, Mexican, 16, 101, 118, 121, 124–25
Liberia, 97
Lincoln, Abraham: American Indian policies of, 154–55; diplomatic ability of, 14, 58; and emancipation, 17, 33, 131–32; and Emancipation Proclamation, 42–43; on European implications of emancipation, 141, 143; and Great Britain, 31, 42; ideology of, 58, 65n. 24, 131–33, 148; and recognition of Confederacy, 3; Russian minister's impression of, 139; second annual message of, 131–32; and Seward, 58; and St. Albans Raid, 9. *See also* Great Britain: image of Lincoln in